The Shaping of God's People:
One Story of How God is Shaping the North American Church Through Short Term Missions

Craig Altrock, D.Min.

Copyright 2006 by Craig Altrock

Self published at www.LuLu.com

All rights reserved. No part of this publication may be reproduced, stored in a retrieval system, or transmitted in any form or by any means- for example, electronic, photocopy, recording- without the prior written permission of the author. The only exception is brief quotations in printed reviews.

ISBN 978-0-6151-6895-1

Contents

Introduction 5

Chapter One: Shaping the Missionary Heart of the Worker 17

    Change in Missional Scripture Reading 18
    Change in Missional Prayer Life 21
    Change in Missional View of God... 22
    Change in Missional View of Self... 23

Chapter Two: Molding the Missionary Hands of the Worker 25

    Change in Local Mission Involvement.. 27
    Change in Mission Giving 27
    Anything Good in Missions Happening Locally? 28

Chapter Three: Forming the Missionary Commitment of the Worker 31

    Involvement in Ongoing Missions.. 32
    Plans to Participate in Long-Term Missions..................................... 33

Chapter Four: The Theological Lens – Coming Home "Sent"... 35

    The Theme of Mission in the Gospel of John.................................. 36
    The Theme of Sending in John 17 and 20 38
    The Sending Motif Throughout John.. 39
    Theological Implications 42
        Seeking Activity That Reflects Our "Sent" Nature 43
        Seeing All Activity Through A Missional Lens 43
        Seeing Ourselves as Missionaries.. 44
        Stepping Into Our Community 44
        Seizing Our Identity From the Proper Source............................. 45

Chapter Five: Implications 47

    Acknowledging the Power of Ministry to Shape.............................. 48
    The Ripple Effect at Home 49
    Bridging Short-Term and Long-Term 53

Keeping High Standards 54
Changing Our Minds.. 54

Chapter Six: Training... 57

Backing into Your Training 61
Training Areas 63
   Independence Verses Dependence.. 63
   Objectives and Expectations of the Work On-Site 66
   Personal Qualities 67
   Long-term nature of our short-term work................................... 68

Chapter Seven: Conclusion 71

Questions for further study 72
Closing Comments 74

Appendix: Exegetical issues related to the theme of sending in John 20:19-23 77

Introduction

"When people spoke about missions at church, I tuned out-quickly. I came from a background where I wasn't a big supporter of missions." Zane approached missions skeptically for the first 43 years of his life. There were enough needy people at home, and he wanted no part of contributing to someone's mission "vacation." Then his wife Melissa participated in a Let's Start Talking short-term mission project. When she returned from a three week project to Japan she said to her husband, *"Let's sell our home."* She suggested a major downsizing so they could afford to do more mission work at home and abroad. Zane agreed and then traveled on his own LST project; the first mission project in his life. *"When I got back home I felt like had been re-grounded and reset. It was very clear to me what was important and what was trivia."* Today Zane is the head of the missions committee at his home congregation, and his wife Melissa helps lead an outreach to international people in their neighborhood. If you ask them what prompted this radical downsizing and renewed vigor in local and international evangelism they will say, *"My LST project."*

One million people now participate in short-term missions annually.[1] God is weaving this form of mission work is into the ministry-fabric of the North American church as a means of assisting mission congregations in other countries and releasing the energies and talents of North American Christians with a desire to serve worldwide. What we now call Short-Term Missions is as old as the journeys of Paul, is stationed as a significant force in 21st century missions, and yet remains little understood by most.

- What are the true effects of short-term missions?

---

[1] Ken Walker, "Agencies Announce Short-Term Missions Standards," *Christianity Today* (October 2003), [article on-line]; available from http://www.christianitytoday.com/ct/2003/010/19.30.html; Internet; accessed 29 August 2004. Other estimates put the number of participants even higher!

- What can we know about this mission force that goes beyond mere anecdotal evidence?

- What evidence do we have to further support the advancement of this missions venue while critically seeking to improve its methods, focus, and character?

This study examines one side of the short-term mission equation- What are the effects of short-term missions on those who go? More specifically, we inspect the perceived influence of short-term mission experience through the Let's Start Talking Ministry (LST) on its workers with regard to the missional aspects of their lives in the local congregation, their involvement with or participation in further mission work, and their personal/spiritual development missionally.[2]

This is not a study to simply answer the question of "What happens to workers who go on short-term projects?" The focus of our exploration is more specific. We are looking at how such experience shapes North American workers (and their congregations) in terms of missions.

- Does this experience change the way those who go see themselves in missions, see God as a missionary God, read Scripture missionally, or even pray for missions?

- Do short-term missions shape the worker's actions at their home congregation when they return? Are they more or less

---

[2] At the time of this writing, the term "missional" is an increasingly popular way to talk about the missionary nature of a church and/or its members (this can be seen in the growing area of missional church literature). For a good definition of "missional" as well as one example of the difference between missional churches and churches with mission programs, see The Center for Parish Development, "Is 'Missional' A Real Word?" and "What is the Difference Between a Missional Church and a Church with a Mission Program?" [article on-line]; available from http://www.missionalchurch.org/pages/faq.pdf; Internet; accessed 2 January 2006.

likely to become involved in mission-oriented works when they return? Will these workers support missions with increased vigor?

- How likely are short-term workers to strongly consider either supporting long-term missions at a higher level or becoming more involved themselves in long-term missions as a result of their short-term experience?

These are the kinds of questions this study answers. We are attempting to drill down into the lives and commitment of Christians who have experienced God's global work through short-term missions.

Having said that, Christians should not go on short-term missions simply because of what they can gain from the experience. This perspective lacks a long-term vision, promotes a self-centered form of Christian service, and eventually serves little purpose except to manipulate non-Christians on a mission field for the sole purpose of pleasing North American Christians. Christian service, regardless of its duration or location, is about God and not about us. But, the assertion often heard in mission circles that short-term missions are almost always better for those who go than for those we seek to reach doesn't have to be a true assertion.

One important factor in examining the importance of short-term missions is understanding the true impact these projects make on-site. This is a crucial question for anyone involved in mission work. However, to keep our study focused and concise, we will spotlight this singular issue - how God is using short-term missions to shape the North American church, to increase it's enthusiasm for long-term missions, and to equip it to reach into it's own mission context at home.

The results of this study are based on the experiences of Let's Start Talking alumni. The Let's Start Talking Ministry (LST) is a missions ministry among churches of Christ. This ministry has served our fellowship for over twenty-five years by recruiting, training and sending out groups of Christians to share their faith and themselves in mission settings both around the world and in the U.S. LST workers help interested nationals/internationals practice conversational English using Scripture as text. Internationally, LST projects vary in length from one week to one year, with the bulk of the work accomplished by six-week teams. Domestic Churches of Christ use LST in longer-term ministries to serve non-native English speakers in their neighborhoods.

LST has served increasing numbers of individuals and churches since 1981. Over 2,500 Christians have participated in short-term projects through LST since its inception. In 2005 LST sent out more than 500 workers to more twenty-five countries on over one hundred mission projects. Because of the long history LST shares as well as the number of people who have served on LST projects, this ministry provides a rich arena for learning about short-term missions.

Our findings are rooted in two streams of data. First, during 2003 and 2004 we interviewed thirty-four LST alum in three separate groups. We based these groups on a specific demographic paradigm and the length of time that had passed since their first LST project. Group one included those who participated in their first LST project one to six months from the time of the study, group two were those who participated in their first project six to twenty-four months from the time of the study, and the last group were those who participated in their first project twenty-four to forty-eight months from the time of the study. Because past experience, socio-economic background, age, and education of LST workers is so varied, we used 2002 LST alumni demographics as a demographic paradigm for whom to interview (how many men, how many who were 18-22, etc.).

The second stream of data comes from an on-line survey we sent to LST alum in 2004. We initially sent the inquiry to a list of 1,233 LST alumni for whom we had e-mail addresses (as of the end of 2003, we had about 2,100 total Alumni). At the close of the survey 414 had responded. This gave a 50% response rate of possible responses (50% of the 822 total possible responses (the number of good e-mail addresses we had for LST alum)), or a 35% response rate of all LST alumni.

While we will explore in depth each of the change areas these short-term workers reported, we think it might be helpful for you to have an overall glimpse at the results. The graphics below register the percentage of respondents who indicated a positive change in response to each question.

1. Positive change in missional Scripture reading

Has your LST experience affected your reading of Scripture in the area of missions? For example, has this experience affected your reading of Scripture as it relates to God being a missionary God? Has it caused you to see certain stories in a new light, to see mission themes in Scripture in new ways, etc.?

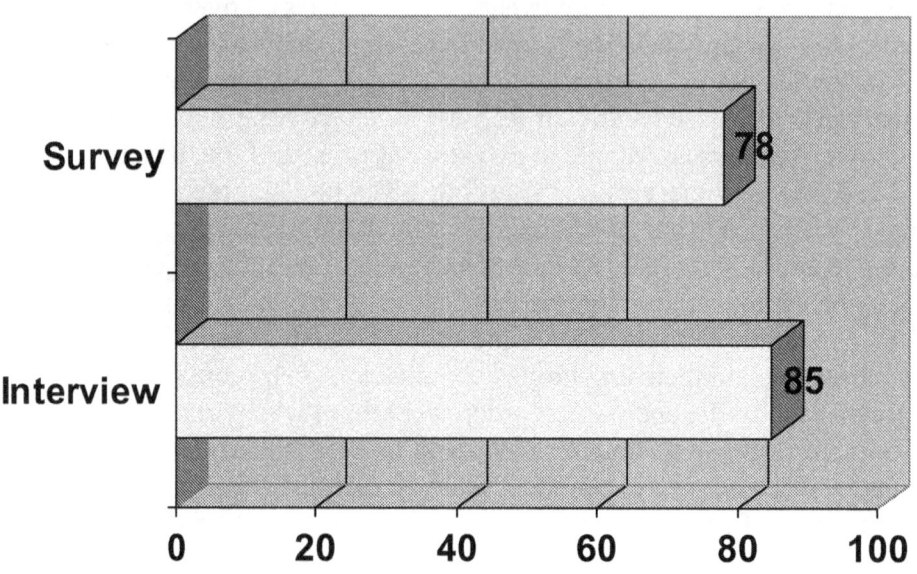

2. Positive change in missional prayer life

Has this experience affected your personal prayer life in the area of missions? For example, has this experience affected your personal prayer life as it relates to God's concern for the world, as it relates to whom you pray for, as it relates to how you pray for mission work, as it relates to the time you spend in prayer for missions? Are your prayers more focused in terms of praying for specific missionaries, geographical locations, people groups, countries, etc?

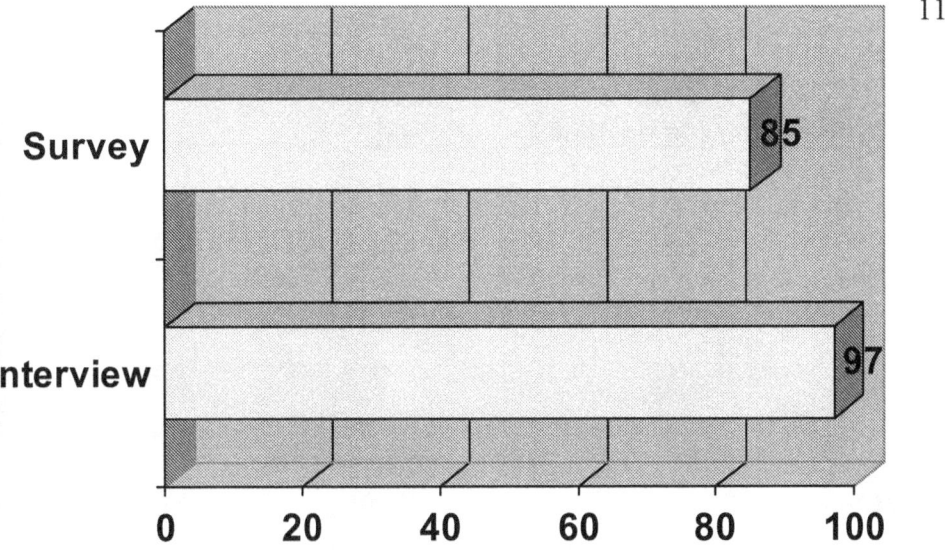

3. Positive change in missional view of God

Has this experience affected your foundational understanding of God as it relates to missions? For example, did it help you see God as more of a global God? Did it help you see how God works in other cultures?

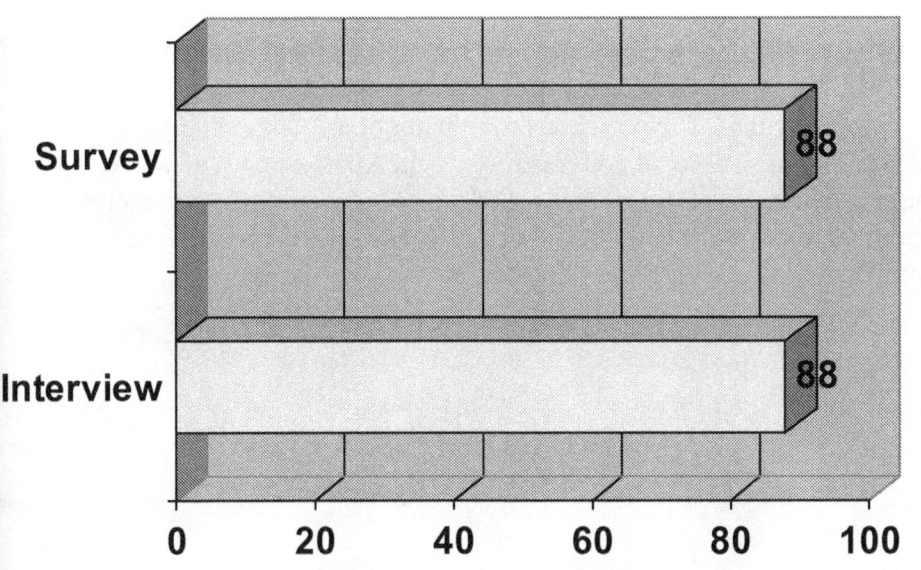

4. Positive change in missional view of self

Has this experience affected your view and understanding of yourself in the area of missions? For example, would there be a difference about your view and understanding of yourself spiritually in the area of missions had you not gone on an LST project?

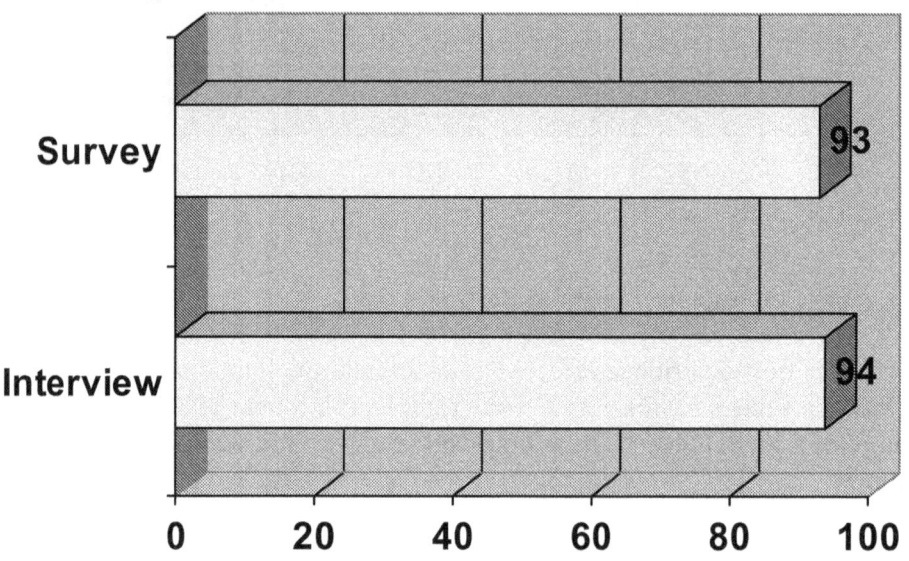

5. Positive change in missional involvement in local church

Has your LST experience brought about any change in your involvement at your local congregation in the kinds of activities you would consider mission-oriented? Examples might include outreach to internationals, speaking about missions, local evangelism, mission committee work, writing missionaries, etc.

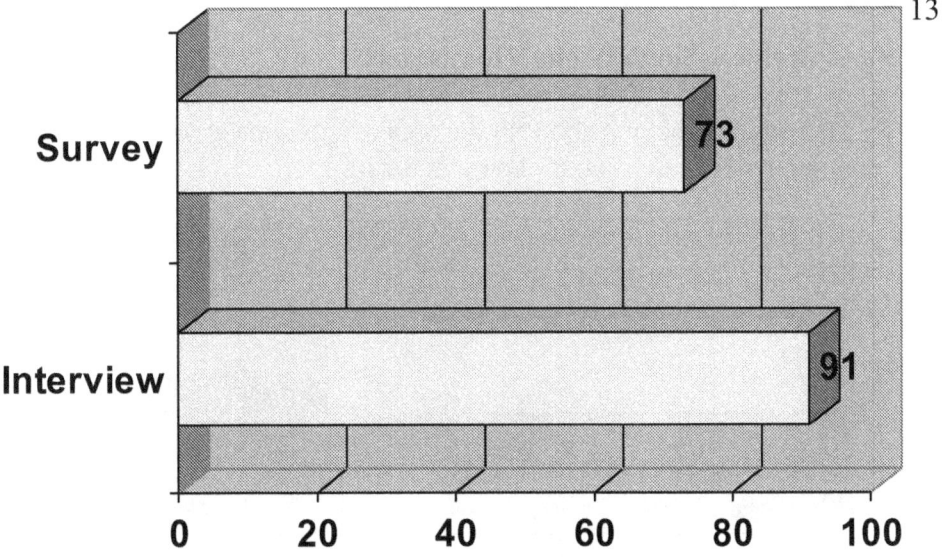

6. Positive change in giving more to missions

Has your LST experience influenced the way in which you give financially to missions at your local congregation? Because of your LST experience are you giving more to missions, more regularly to missions, have you made any changes in terms of the kinds of people you give to, etc.?

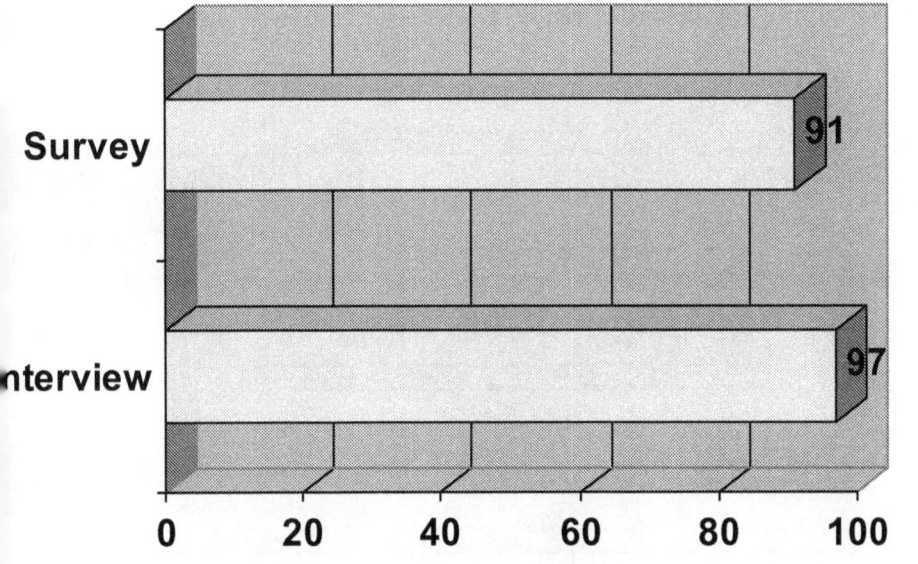

7. Positive change in local church missions

Has any good come about in the area of missions at your local congregation as a result of your experience with LST?

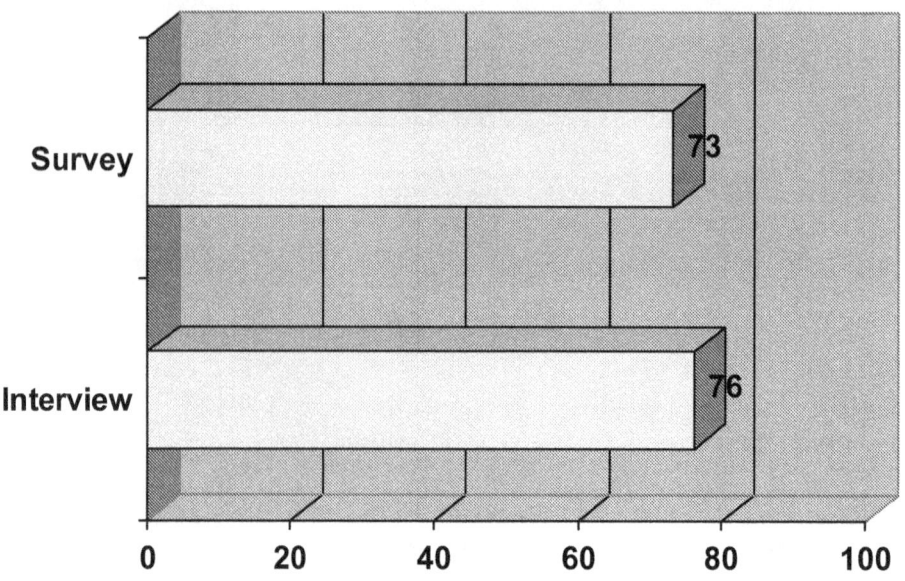

8. Positive change in involvement in long-term missions

Has your LST experience affected your involvement with or in ongoing mission work? (Involvement might include going, helping send ($), supporting through prayer, etc.)

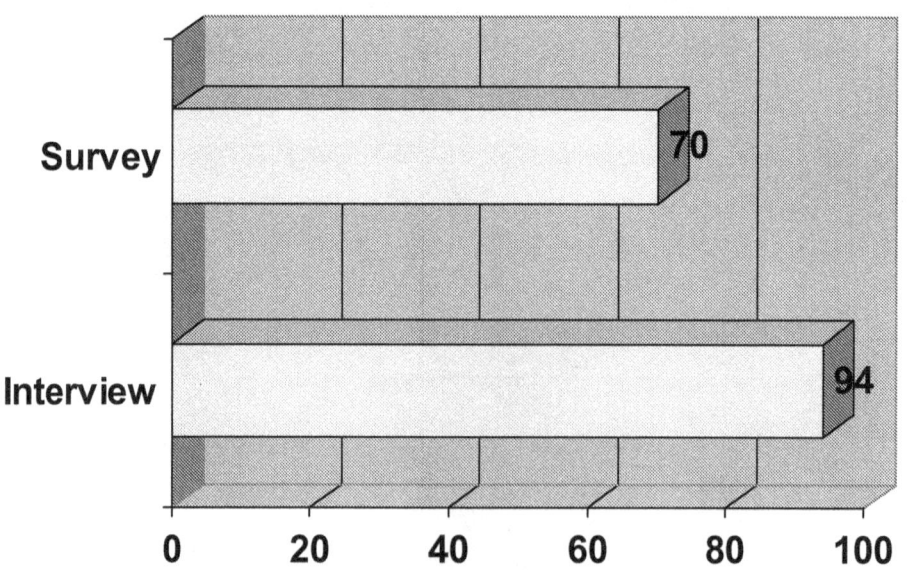

9. Have participated in another short-term project since first LST project?

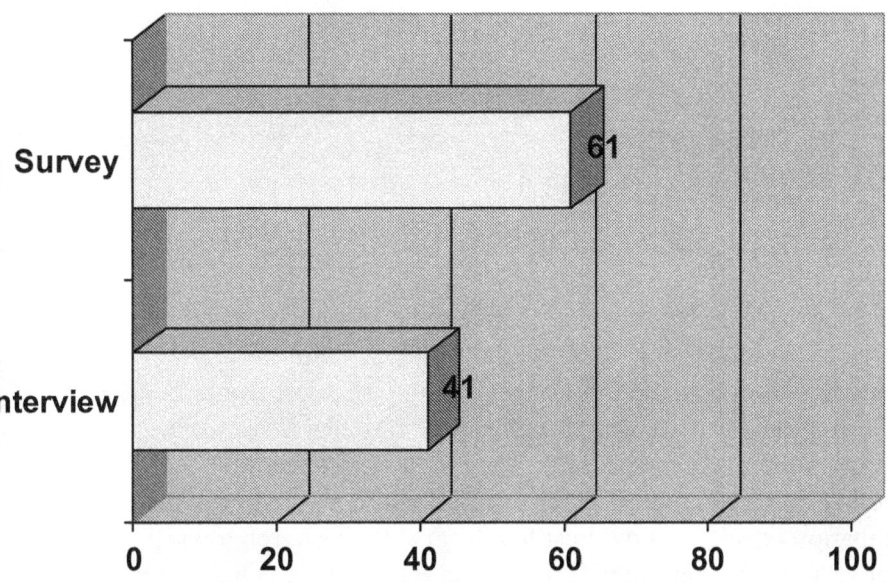

10. Participation in long-term missions

Have you participated or do you have plans to participate in ongoing/long-term mission work as a result of your LST experience?

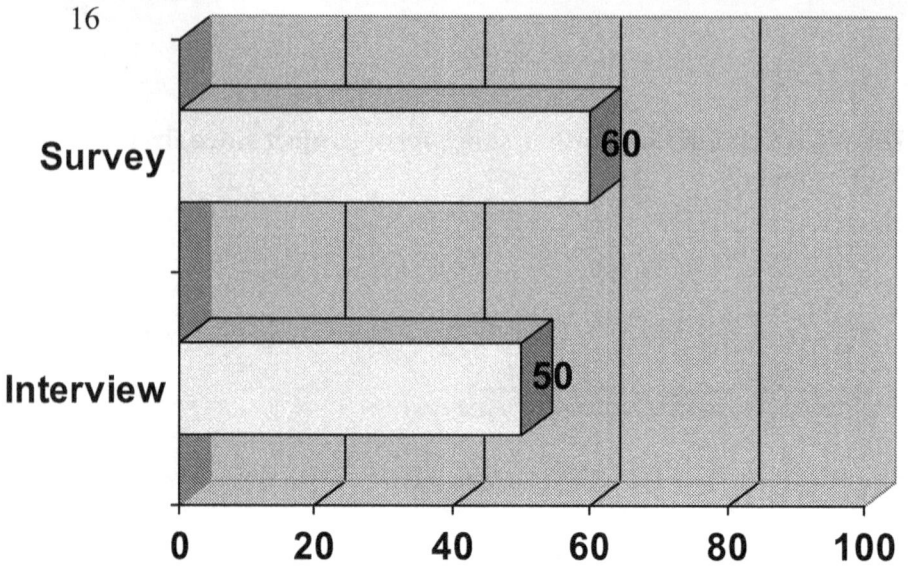

This book is for anyone seeking to understand or become more involved in mission work. It is for the missions committee chair person who sits with a plethora of requests for support from potential short-term missions workers. It is for the long-term missionary pondering the need for short-term workers to come from his supporting congregation. It is for the leadership team at growing congregations deciding how best to energize their church toward greater service and outreach. It is for the short-term worker tentatively deciding whether to spend a summer or even a year on-site.

We open this window into short-term missions and its workers with great optimism and anticipation. Be encouraged at how God is shaping the North American church to be even more reflective of her missionary nature. Think critically with us about how to make this tool even more effective in the feeble hands of those whom God sends. Look at what God is doing, and think of what more he could do if we would only ask him!

Chapter One: Shaping the Missionary Heart of the Worker

Quotes from the Field[3]

In large ways and small, LST has affected the way I see myself in the area of missions. I see my life as less of an end, and more of a means; a means that can be used by God to see more of the world saved.

I NEVER thought I would be a missionary. I NEVER thought I would even consider that as a life choice. I didn't think I had that potential to be a missionary. But going on a LST project has opened that door for me and I consider full-time mission work as a possibility for me in the future.

Our God is huge. It is impossible for the human mind to imagine God as big as He really is. He is not confined to one congregation. He is not confined to one country. My LST project opened my eyes to see that God is alive and at work everywhere! Some of the most encouraging and inspiring Christians I have met lived in countries in which Christians were greatly oppressed. Our God is just. He is good. He gives to people what they need to follow Him.

---

[3] These "Quotes From the Field" sections record the words of short-term workers who participated in this study. These are their actual words concerning their experiences.

Sarah was 26 years old when she participated in her first LST project. If you ask her why she signed up to go initially, Sarah will say, *"I still don't really understand what made me sign up to do this, in the first place. I've never felt that missions was something that I could do, or something that was my gift."* Yet Sarah went. She endured the training. She applied for a passport. She wrote fundraising letters. And she shared her faith, the best way she knew how. What changed for Sarah as a result of this project? She is convicted that despite her best intuition at the front-end of the project, God does have a call on her life for missions. In fact Sarah will tell you that God has a call on all Christians – we are all missionaries. *"I mean, that was a huge mental change for my brain in that this is something that God calls me to do even if I didn't think I was made for it... in some respect, everyone can do it. We still may not all be able to go out on the street corner and preach, but mission work comes along in a lot of different ways and God calls us each to do it."* Today you can find Sarah teaching local children at a Christian school in the Philippines!

What is God doing to the heart and perception of the short-term worker through their experiences? Does sharing in God's work in a cross-cultural setting change anything about our own heart? Is Sarah's experience simply anecdotal? This is first area our study examines. We will look at whether short-term mission experience shapes reading of Scripture in the area of missions, personal prayer life in the area of missions, understanding of God in the area of missions, and understanding of self in the area of missions.

Change in Missional Scripture Reading

God uses LST mission experience to positively affect missional reading of Scripture. Twenty-nine of the thirty-four who were interviewed and 78% of those surveyed indicated some type of positive change in their reading of Scripture from a missionary or missional point of view. As a result of serving God in a mission field workers were reading their Bibles differently. While many stated that the experience had positively affected their *missionary* reading of

Scripture, other positive changes such as the following were noted, too:

- Reading Scripture as if they had never read it before,

- Seeing old Scriptures in new light,

- Gaining skills in how to share Scripture,

- Obtaining new models for ministry that were rooted in Scripture (For example, the Parable of the sower and the principle that God's Word is the teacher (I don't have to be the teacher!)),

- Realizing through Scripture that God is calling them to go into the world,

- Identifying with certain Biblical character more readily.

One of the themes that is repeated several times is how powerful God's word is. The LST project placed workers in an environment where the powerful influence of God's word became evident to them.

LST workers identify two elements that are responsible in part for the large number of positive changes in the way they read their Bibles now. One part of the experience that aided this change was the cross-cultural setting of their reading. Seeing Scripture through the eyes of someone from another culture brought about a positive change in the way these North American Christians now read Scripture. The other item mentioned is reading Scripture with a non-Christian. This, too, produced a positive change in the way LST workers themselves read Scripture.

Many specific Scriptures are mentioned in the interviews. However, three are noted prominently. Participants mention the parable of the sower and the seed as a new model for understanding ministry and how God works in the lives of people. The story of Jesus and the Samaritan woman arises as an example of a cross-cultural encounter Jesus experienced where he exhibited great compassion on someone culturally different. Last, some respondents noted the story of the wise and foolish builder as a good example of a well-known story which they learned to see in a new light as a result of reading Scripture during their LST project.

Two additional items stand out. First, there are a number of LST participants who indicate a change in some skill as a result of reading Scripture on an LST project. This is surprising since the study itself did not seek that kind of information. Skills mentioned include the following:

- Having new themes/Scriptures to share with non-Christians in meaningful ways.

- Being able to talk about God with people from non-Christian religions.

- Having a new way (real stories) to talk about missions in our churches.

- Having a cultural sensitivity to using Scripture.

- Obtaining a new model for ministering to the lost (the seed-planting analogy and Word-is-the-teacher paradigm we use in our LST training) that is focused more on the quality of conversion than the quantity of conversions.

- Having the ability to speak about God without using Christian "lingo."

- Taking with them from the project a new way of fulfilling the Great Commission.

Second, a relatively large group indicated a positive theological change as a result of reading Scripture on their LST projects. Reading Scripture in this way brought about a change for them in how they understood God. Examples of this theological shift include the following:

- God could and would enrich their speaking so they could answer difficult questions.

- Participants gained a deeper understanding how God is working in the world. They understood that God wants everybody to be part of his family.

- LST workers learned better the kinds of "barriers" Christ went through as he relinquished a place in heaven to set his feet on earth. A new appreciation grew for the power of God's word. Project workers understood better that God is the only one who can bring about life-change. God's mission in the world will not fail, regardless of the challenges.

Change in Missional Prayer Life

According to participants, LST project experience affected their personal prayer life in the area of missions. Thirty-three of the thirty-four interviewed and 85% of those surveyed indicated some sort of positive change in their prayer life (in the area of missions). More so than in the first question, here respondents were easily able to identify not only changes in their prayer life, but changes in how they prayed for missions. Virtually every person who indicated a positive change meant that the change was in terms of how they pray for missions.

The most often mentioned change in their prayer life was that now they could be more specific. They had specific places in mind. They had faces and names.[4]

A surprising finding here concerns the number of people who indicated some kind of skill or behavior change. Twenty-four of the thirty-four interviewed indicate the adoption of a new skill in their prayer life as a result of their LST experience. Twenty-eight of the

---

[4] Several other items were mentioned as part of the change that had occurred in their missional prayers. Participants mention understanding better the role of prayer in fundraising. They are more likely to pray for other things going on in the world instead of just praying for what is happening at home. Their prayer life has a more global perspective. They experienced the importance of praying for missionaries. They witnessed the role of prayer in preparing people's hearts to receive God's word.

thirty-four noted changed behavior in their prayer life as a result of their project.[5]

Change in Missional View of God

As with the question about Scripture reading, this question brought a rich variety of answers and insight. Thirty of the thirty-four interviewed and 88% of those surveyed indicated a positive change in their foundational understanding of God as it relates to missions. God used the experience to shape their understanding of him!

LST experience has strong influence on changing participants' theology. We see this here as well as in the answers about Scripture reading. The role of experience in shaping theology is worth noting and will be something to which we will return. LST workers gave several examples of how their thinking about God had changed as a result of their LST experience. Their quotes give us insight into this changed way of thinking about God:

God is at work all over the world. Just as much as God can work in America, he can work any other place and every other place.

I now see God's love is global. He is not only at work, but he loves people outside of my country.

He loves my new friends in other places as much as he loves me here in my place.

I now see that God is the kind of God who wants to use every child of his to help reach the lost.

---

[5] I would summarize the acquisition of skill by saying that a large group of LST participants no longer have to make the statement, "I just don't know how to pray for missions, for missionaries, or for lost people." These workers know now how to form these kinds of prayers and they have specifics to pray about. Almost everyone who indicated such a skill acquisition had also made behavioral changes in their prayer life. They pray for specific lost people, actual missionaries, and known mission sites.

God's family is communal and that community exists every where he is at work.

God has his own timing and will work as he wills.

God is willing and pleased to accept the worship and worship practices of people from other cultures who approach him in culturally relevant ways.

God showed these LST workers that his church might look different in different places, and that these differences merely reflect his love for all people.

Change in Missional View of Self

A majority of those interviewed and 93% of those surveyed indicate that their LST experience brought about a positive change in terms of how they viewed themselves in the area of missions. One of the misconceptions or critiques of short-term missions is that they only serve to effect change in the life of those who go. This question in our study was worded to steer away from general comments about how "this mission trip changed my life." Instead, the question aims only at identifying a perceived change in terms of how they view themselves in the area of missions.

Responses were many and varied in explaining the kind of change that took place. A majority of responses can be summed up in a new sense of confidence expressed in the statement, "I can do this!"

LST participants do not necessarily see mission work as easy, or that they are somehow ready now to plant a church. The bottom line for many of these workers is a new belief that there is a place for them in missions. What had seemed to them to be almost impossible (doing mission work) was much more of a reality now. Balancing this new-found courage and sense of ability was a more realistic understanding of what they could actually expect to accomplish on the field.

Another explanation for the changed identity is the acquisition of some new skill. Several gave responses that imply they gained a new skill that was enabling them for the first time to think that God could use them for missions.[6]

God is shaping the hearts of his people through this short-term service. These workers are reading their Bible differently, praying more positively, seeing themselves in a new light, and understanding more of God's heart for the world.

---

[6] Basic skills such as discipline and the ability to speak about Christ without having to know all the answers or being afraid of what that person might say are mentioned. Other changes mentioned include the following: Participants understood better what their role in conversion was and what God's role is. God's powerful use of his word is mentioned as a new concept learned. The revelation that significant ministry can occur in just six weeks on the field. I realize now that I am materialistic. Mission work is not only something that happens overseas; it can occur at home too. The only person who indicated a negative change was one known to have had a very difficult project. There may be a connection here between having a negative experience and having a negative perception about yourself on the field. On the other hand, I have seen many LST workers who had very tough projects who left their project with a very strong positive change in terms of how they viewed themselves in the area of missions.

Chapter Two: Molding the Missionary Hands of the Worker

Quotes from the Field

Even three years after my first LST trip, I had an interest in reaching out to the Hispanic population located around our church building. Most likely I would not have had the desire to do that before my LST project. I was also on the mission committee at this church which was a direct result of my mission experience. I'm much more passionate now about long term and short term mission work and where we (the church) can get more money to fund things like this.

I am empathetic with people who shyly ask for money to further God's kingdom. I am a lot more giving with my money. I now have a better understanding of how my money is really just God's money. I want to help whoever I can take mission trips.

Our church now supports a family in Rio de Janeiro who first decided to become missionaries there because of an LST campaign. Another couple from our congregation are also missionaries there in Rio, having first experienced missions through LST. The congregation is also overseeing my work in Prague, which also started with LST. Every year at least one team from our church's campus ministry does an LST campaign, and it seems like every year someone considers a life of ministry as a result. I know two guys now in campus ministry, a girl who wants to be a missionary in Mexico, another girl who wants to be a missionary anywhere, and another guy who goes on LST every year... all because they went the first time on a campaign and God changed their lives through it.

George participated in his first LST project as a 69 year old elder at his local congregation. He traveled all over the world in the Air Force and had participated in one other short-term mission project, but this was his first experience with LST. He journeyed to Buenos Aires for six weeks and returned there several times in subsequent years. As an elder, we might wonder what kind of impact his experience had on the church over which he served. Here are his conclusions:

- The congregation began a new outreach to international students at the local university, and thirty percent of the 200 member congregation participated in this new ministry.

- Giving increased from $800-$900 per year for missions to $5,000-$8,000 per year.

- At one point after his LST experience he wanted to step down as an elder. His fellow elders refused to let him because his involvement in missions was such an example to the congregation they couldn't afford for him not to continue leading.

- George became a leader on the missions committee at his congregation

- He has also helped other area congregations start reaching out to the international population in their neighborhoods.

What is God doing in the lives of short-term workers when they return to their home congregations? What kind of involvement do they have in mission-oriented activities at home? Does their giving to missions increase? In this chapter we'll explore just how characteristic George's story is of others who participate in short-term missions.

Change in Local Mission Involvement

Workers returning home from their LST projects are becoming more involved in missions at home. Thirty-one of thirty-four interviewed and 73% of those surveyed indicated a positive change in actual involvement with missions at a local level. The most oft-mentioned change is a behavior change. LST participants are coming home and actually changing their behavior in terms of involvement at their local setting (church, campus ministry, school) in the kinds of activities they consider mission-oriented.

Two of the largest areas where these Christians are changing their behavior include involvement in outreach to international friends at home and participation in a missions committee. Many LST participants interviewed state that one of the first things they did upon return was either start a FriendSpeak ministry (the name of LST's domestic ministry), join an existing one, or do something to better interact with internationals in their neighborhood. Additionally, six out of thirty-four interviewed mention their current involvement on missions committees as a direct result of their participation on an LST project.

Several other areas of behavior change are mentioned. As a result of their LST project, participants were involved in Missions Sunday promotions and collections, changed their college majors, spoke out more about missions than before they went, made decisions to work in an inner city church, and decided to go into long-term missions (domestic and foreign).

Clearly not every participant indicated a positive change in their state-side behavior. Those who indicated no change were either already involved in mission-oriented activities, simply had not found a way to become more involved, or had other kinds of ministries for which they shared greater passion.

Change in Mission Giving

As in the previous question, a majority of those interviewed indicated a positive change, and that change was a change in behavior. Twenty-six of thirty-four who were interviewed and 73% of those surveyed stated that they had a positive change in terms of giving to missions.

We should make two important notes before going further. First, it is important to see that the behavior change was not always an increase in giving at a local congregation. Some of the increases in giving were due to making additional contributions to specific individuals or entities raising mission funds outside of the local setting. Second, the study would have been deepened if we had asked about any changes in attitude toward giving. This does come out in some of the responses, however most interviewees understood the question to deal only with actual giving.

The largest change in behavior noted by these Christians was an increase in giving. Some gave more to their local church, others were now supporting specific individuals doing mission work, and still others were giving more to outside mission.

Accompanying a change in behavior is a changed perspective. At some level they had a new attitude about giving to missions. This attitude is largely summed up in the idea that they were much more open and sensitive to give when they received a funding request for missions. Their own experience had sensitized them to the need to give and the difficulty involved in raising mission funds.

Anything Good in Missions Happening Locally?

This question opened the door for participants to mention anything else they could think of that was happening in the area of missions at their local congregation (or school/campus ministry) that was a result of their LST project. Thirty-two of thirty-four interviewees and 70% of those surveyed reported a positive change. Many beneficial things were happening in the area of mission at their local congregation which these participants linked to their own LST project experience.

Besides the kinds of things mentioned in response to the first two questions in this area, those interviewed revealed a wide range of ways in which their local congregation was being influenced for good as a result of their personal LST project experience.

- The eyes of their churches were opened up to missions.

- They were more interested in missions and in local evangelism.

- Several congregations had begun FriendSpeak ministries.

- Some reported an increased courage among congregational members to consider doing short-term missions, while others indicated more people were now doing short-term missions.

- One new staff position in the area of missions was being considered.

- Some churches now had new missionaries to support because of the relationship built with that missionary during an LST project.

- Missions committees are more informed and have new members as a result of LST projects.

- Churches have better relationships with their missionaries.

- Missions giving has increased.

- Prior LST participants are stepping into new areas of leadership at their congregations.

- There is a new emphasis in some churches on team work in ministry and missions.

- Their congregation now has a positive view of LST and its programs.

    We should not overstate the case. Some of the reported changes are incremental in nature and may be as small as simply a renewed interest in missions. Other changes reported, however, have a seemingly larger impact. Taken together with the first two questions from this area, we gain a good picture of how LST projects influence the local settings of participants (at least from their perspective).
    God is shaping not only the hearts of those who go, but in response to their faithful service in a separate culture, he is molding their hands so that they become more involved at home in missions as well.

Chapter Three: Forming the Missionary Commitment of the Worker

Quotes from the Field

...I am now a full-time field worker, in one of the cities where I did an LST project five years ago. I think that's a big impact!

I have decided to participate in future summer mission trips to new areas to see faith displayed in even more cultures. I am considering becoming a missionary because of my involvement with LST.

My LST experiences made me so much more mindful of the mission work that other people do. I think it's probably one of the most important things Christians do, and I'm committed to being a part of it in any way that I can.

"*My LST experience changed the course of my life.*" Mallissa was 28 years old, studying public relations, and completing a Master's Degree. Before graduating and getting into full time work, Mallissa decided to take a summer and do some mission work. She ventured into Brazil with LST. After coming home she started studying missions. Six months later she was part of the mission committee at her local congregation. "*And I feel like I had a really significant impact on the committee and on the church in general because I was able to offer up my perspective and was one of the people that wrote the missions policy and guidelines for the church.*" But that wasn't the end of God's work in her life. Reflecting on her experience with LST, being involved on the missions committee, and studying about missions brought about a complete change in trajectory for Mallissa. Two years after returning from Brazil, the missions committee that Mallissa had joined sent *her* as a full-time missionary to Bronx, New York. What began as a simple desire to do some mission work for one summer bloomed into a desire to serve full-time on the mission field.

God shapes the heart of the worker to make them more sensitive and in tune with His missionary character. God molds the hands of the worker so that they return ready to plant seeds in their own neighborhood. What happens to the missionary commitment of the worker? Do returning workers like Mallissa see themselves as more involved in long-term mission work as a result of their experience? This is the main question we'll look at in this chapter.

Involvement in Ongoing Missions

LST project participants indicate that their experience with LST does affect involvement with or in ongoing mission work. Thirty-three of thirty-four interviewed and 91% of those surveyed make statements showing a positive change in their involvement with ongoing mission work. Those participating in LST projects come home and make changes in their behavior in relation to their involvement in ongoing mission work. The types of changed behaviors noted vary widely.

- Some have made commitments to do long-term mission work, while others are already doing it. Both tie that decision back to having done LST.

- Many mention praying more and praying specifically in the area of missions.

- More communication is taking place with existing missionaries with the intent of encouraging them.

- Giving to missions in general has increased in some places, others have picked up the support of new missionaries they met on their LST projects, and others are giving from a more informed (and critical) standpoint.

- A few respondents see themselves as supporting long-term mission through going again on short-term missions.

- Last, as in previous questions, those interviewed tie their current involvement with missions committees or in FriendSpeak works to their prior LST experience.

We need to be clear here that the reported positive change does not necessarily mean a majority of LST workers are giving more money for missions at their local church or that they are all now making decisions to join long-term efforts (two areas that might stereotypically represent ways people increase their involvement in long-term missions). The responses indicate 1) that LST participants have a broad understanding of what "involvement in ongoing mission work" involves, and that 2) for some LST workers their experience did indeed lead them toward increased financial giving or toward actually going into the field long-term. Several workers indicate a broadened understanding of what constitutes a mission field, so that they view their own work (even if it is state-side) as mission work.

Plans to Participate in Long-Term Missions

In some ways this question mimics the one asked above. The question tries to be more specific, however, in asking whether the participant intends to "participate" in ongoing or long-term mission work as a result of their LST experience. As we noticed above, LST participants have a wide view of what involvement in ongoing mission work might include, and while relatively small in any given year, there is a group of them who do end up actually going on the field to do long term work.

Interestingly, more people indicated they had plans to participate or were participating in long-term mission work as a result of their LST experience than indicated they had participated in a short-term project as a result of their LST experience. Seventeen respondents answered this question positively. They were either currently involved in long-term mission work or had plans to be involved. Fifty percent of those interviewed and 60% of those surveyed fit in this category.

Again, we should not overstate the case. This does not mean that fifty percent of those surveyed were in fact on the field or currently on teams forming to go on the field. It simply means these workers were either actually on the field or they had some sort of plan to be on the field in the future.

What must be encouraged by the fact that short-term workers are returning home with a sense of the long-term need in missions and a heightened commitment to participate in that need. Rather than creating a bunch of short-term mission groupies, these experiences are shaping people's long-term commitments!

Chapter Four: The Theological Lens – Coming Home "Sent"

Quotes from the Field

"I think for the first time in my life I actually came back and thought, 'I could be a missionary.'"

Bob was a full-time minister with preaching experience in Indiana and Oklahoma. He preached and taught every Sunday for decades. He regularly counseled with people using the Bible as a guide. Yet he was 54 years old when he did his first mission project with LST. Like others you've met in previous chapters, God moved in Bob's heart during his short-term mission experience. One of the most significant changes Bob experienced was a sense of being sent. *"I think for the first time in my life I actually came back and thought, 'I could be a missionary.'. I felt, and still, two-and-a-half years later feel like that's something that I felt through LST; a call ... a feeling of 'Oh, this would be more in line with what you really love to do.' I never had felt that before, and I think LST planted those seeds in me."*

With the results of the previous chapters before us, we must back up and ask what God is seeing through his perspective. How would God interpret these results? If he were sitting down with us as we measured the results of short-term experience on those who go, what words would he offer us? What kind of lens does theology offer to us as we explore these issues?

God is a sending God and his people are a sent people. Just as God sent Jesus into the world, so today he sends his church into the world. As Bob concluded from his short-term experience, God desires his people to shape their identity and mission around the notion that they are sent. Our study of LST participants indicates that short-term missions shape workers around this identity. This chapter will examine the theological pattern of God-as-a-sending-God and relate it to the work of short-term missions.

The Theme of Mission in the Gospel of John

David Bosch notes, "The Christian faith, I submit, is intrinsically missionary."[7] Mission work is not simply a work of the church (something the church *does*), but God's people themselves are intrinsically missional (something the church *is*). This sense of identity is something today's church must recapture.

For sake of space, let's consider this theme as it appears in one section of Scripture; John's Gospel. The theme of sending or being sent finds repeated emphasis throughout the Gospel.[8] Beasley-Murray states that in light of the striking number of times sending language is

---

[7] David J. Bosch, *Transforming Mission: Paradigm Shifts in Theology of Mission,* American Society of Missiology Series, No. 16 (Maryknoll, NY: Orbis Books, 1991), 8.

[8] While the sending motif in John's Gospel has not found widespread emphasis among scholars, its importance has nonetheless been noted. Authors point to the large occurrence of sending language used in this gospel, to the special way this sending language is used in chapter 17 of John, and the way in which the sending language is used to speak of Jesus as well as Jesus' followers. For an excellent treatment of the mission theme in John see Andreas J. Kostenberger, *The Missions of Jesus and the Disciples According to the Fourth Gospel* (Grand Rapids, MI: Wm. B. Eerdmans, 1998). See especially Johan Ferreira, "Johannine Ecclesiology," *Journal for the Study of the New Testament* Supplement Series 160 (Sheffield, England: Sheffield Academic Press, 1998), 166-200. Martin Erdmann concludes that the theme of mission in John's gospel has been largely ignored by contemporary scholarship, save a number of Catholic scholars. Martin Erdmann, "Mission in John's Gospel and Letters," in *Mission in the New Testament: An Evangelical Approach*, ed. William J. Larkin Jr. and Joel F. Williams (Maryknoll, NY: Orbis Books, 1998), 209. See too Robert Davis Prescott-Ezickson, "The Sending Motif in the Gospel of John: Implications for Theology of Mission" (Ph.D. diss., Southern Baptist Theological Seminary, 1986), 1. As an example, David Alan Black's detailed literary analysis of John 17 does not put any emphasis at all on the theme of sending in John 17 and its relation to the rest of the gospel. David Alan Black, "On the Style and Significance of John 17," *Criswell Theological Review* 3 (Fall 1988): 141-159.

used in John, the contrast with the infrequency of these expressions in the synoptic gospels is "quite extraordinary."[9]

The Theme of Sending in John 17 and 20

The prayer of Jesus in John 17 ends the lengthy upper room dialogue that begins in chapter 13 and extends through chapter 17. As Jesus ends his prayer for his disciples, he speaks to their continuing mission in the world (17:15-19). Just as the Father sent him into the world, so now he is sending his disciples into the world.

Jesus' statement of sending is sandwiched between two verses signifying his desire that God sanctify the disciples, or set them apart for a special purpose. This sanctification is not simply to cleanse the disciples of sin. In John, sanctification or consecration sets one apart for mission in the world. The sending theme in John reaches a crescendo in chapter 17.[10] Jesus is set apart and sent into the world, so now he prays that in the same way God will set the disciples apart and send them into the world.

In Jn. 20:19-23 we see the same theme of sending, but this time coupled with the presence of the Holy Spirit. Here Jesus repeats the commission for the disciples to be sent into the world. As the Father has sent Jesus, so Jesus sends his followers. Again, John emphasizes the parallelism between what the Father has done for Jesus and what

---

[9] G.R. Beasley-Murray, *Gospel of Life: Theology in the Fourth Gospel* (Peabody, MA: Hendrickson, 1991), 15, 16. Leon Morris suggests that of the many ways to understand how John framed his gospel, the theme of sending is one of the ways to interpret what John is getting at in his writing. Leon Morris, *Jesus is the Christ: Studies in the Theology of John* (Grand Rapids: Wm. B. Eerdmans, 1989), 41. To be fair, Morris does not spend much time pursuing this theme in his writing.

[10] Koestenberger, 187. Ferreira, 122; Leon Morris, *The Gospel According to John*, in The New International Commentary on the New Testament (Grand Rapids: Wm. B. Eerdmans, 1971), 300-301. See also Jn. 10:36 and 15:16. This sense of consecration for service is in keeping with the Old Testament understanding (Ex. 28:41).

Jesus is doing for his disciples, and again Jesus underscores his own identity and that of his followers with the idea of "sent."[11]

Some have identified these verses as John's own rendition of the Great Commission.[12] If true, there are strong implications for us. John is not simply telling us that some of us or all of us are to *go* in to the world. All of us are to understand ourselves as *sent*. To "go" implies only an action. To be "sent," however, implies clothing ourselves in a new identity and the lifestyle and priorities which this identity implies.[13]

The Sending Motif Throughout John

What we see in John 17 and 20 is not unique in John. In fact, the sending motif surfaces throughout the entire Gospel. Because this theme is so strong throughout the Gospel it is clear that this theological idea carries much weight for John.

---

[11] Though not of the exact same grammatical construction, the parallelism between what the Father has done for Jesus and what Jesus has done for the disciples is seen in Jn. 6:57, 10:14-15, 15:9, 17:22.

[12] Prescott-Ezickson compares the commissions in the synoptic gospels with Jn. 20:21 and concludes that the commission in John exists but is simply not as clear as in the synoptics. To clarify what John means in his version of the commission, we must understand the theme of sending in his gospel. John Stott calls Jn, 20:21 the crucial form in which the Great Commission has been handed down. Likewise, Bosch assumes Jn. 20:21-23 is John's version of the Great Commission. Prescott-Ezickson, 1; John R.W. Stott, *Christian Mission in the Modern World* (Downers Grove, IL: Intervarsity Press, 1975), 23; Bosch, *Transforming Mission*, 66, 79. The following authors do not explicitly call Jn. 20:21 the Great Commission, but they imply it is indeed John's version of Jesus' commissioning. Beasley-Murray, *Gospel of Life*, 25, 117; Morris, *Jesus is the Christ*, 166-167; Erdman, "Mission in John's Gospel's and Letters," 221-222, and Lesslie Newbigin, *The Light Has Come: An Exposition of the Fourth Gospel* (Grand Rapids: Wm. B. Eerdmans, 1982), 269.

[13] Exegetically, there are a few hurdles in this text. See the appendix for a brief discussion of these issues.

The verbs *pempo* and *apostello* (two worlds meaning "send") are used more often in the Gospel of John than in any other New Testament book. The two words occur sixty times in the Gospel of John (thirty-two and twenty-eight times respectively).[14] The majority of the time in John's gospel God the Father is the one who sends, and Jesus is the one sent. In forty-five occurrences, God is the one sending. In forty occurrences, Jesus is the one sent. There are four locations in the Gospel where the disciples are sent (4:38 [in connection with Jesus' teaching about the fields being ripe], 13:20, 17:18, and 20:21). In three sections the Spirit is sent (14:26, 15:26, and 16:7). The phrase *ho pempsas me* ("the one who sent me") is a formula for John, appearing verbatim nine times.[15] Variations of this same phrase occur an additional fourteen times, making the total occurrences twenty-three.[16] The two verbs are used more times in chapter 17 (seven times) to indicate a missional sending than in any other chapter of the Gospel, and the verbs occur only twice after

---

[14] There is some discussion about whether there exists any substantial difference of meaning between these two verbs in John. Prescott-Ezickson, 65–68 discusses the differences between *pempo* and *apostello*. He notes several authors who either do or do not make a distinction. He suggests that *pempo* is used to demonstrate the relationship between Jesus and the Father, whereas *apostello* is used to show Jesus' relationship to humankind in the mission (p.73). Morris, *Jesus is the Christ*, 103, concludes that John seems to put little difference between these two verbs. He notes that some scholars do make a distinction, but there is no agreement among scholars. He closes by saying, "It is the thought that God has 'sent' the Son that matters, not any precise differentiation between various words for sending." Burge, *The Anointed Community*, 199, also recognizes no significant differences between the two and says they are virtually synonymous in John. So too Kostenberger.

[15] 1:33; 5:37; 6:44; 7:28; 8:16, 18, 26, 29: 12:49. See Johan Ferreira, 192-195 for an analysis of this formula in John. Ferreira counts twenty-four uses of the formula (including variations of the formula) in John's gospel.

[16] These variations are found in 4:34; 5:24, 30; 6:38, 39; 7:16, 33; 9:4; 12:44, 45; 13:20; 14:24; 15:21; 16:5.

chapter 17 in a missional sense (both in 20:21). In the prayer of chapter 17, the phrase *su me apesteilas* ("you sent me") occurs five times (verses 8, 18, 21, 23, 25). Clearly, chapter 17 serves as a crescendo to John's theme of sending.

In addition to the verbs *pempo* and *apostello*, other sending language occurs throughout the Gospel. There are about forty occurrences of other such language. The language describes the Holy Spirit as coming into the world as well as the disciples coming, but most of all it speaks of the coming of Jesus into the world. The presence of such language indicates that John was planting a theological idea, not coincidentally using two or three verbs an unusually large number of times.

Insight into the theology behind the concept of being sent is found in the story of the blind man in John 9. Raymond Brown states that in interpreting the name of the pool as "sent," the Gospel clearly associates the water with Jesus (who was sent).[17] Not understanding that Jesus is sent (or come from heaven) is characteristic of those who are spiritually blind or in the dark (9:39-41). When the church does not understand its own identity as sent (the church derives its identity from that of Jesus), it too remains in the dark.

This additional language of sending is used more times in chapter six (6:25-50) than anywhere else in John. In this section of John, Jesus characterizes himself as the bread of life coming down from heaven.[18] While the stress in John 6:25-50 is on the purpose of Jesus' coming (and his lordship), these verses also underscore the nature of Jesus as having come from heaven into the world (being sent). As Jesus is sent, so too is the church. The church is sent into the world as a provision of life.

It is important in the discussion of this theme in John to observe John's use of the word "world" as he characterizes Jesus and the church as being sent *into the world*. The word *cosmos* ("world") is

---

[17] Raymond Brown, *The Gospel According to John (I-XII)*, The Anchor Bible (Garden City, NY: Doubleday and Co., 1970), 381.

[18] Manna for Israel represented a provision of life for God's people, a test of their obedience, and a way in which Israel could know that the Lord was their God (Ex. 16:3-4, 12). Manna is the bread of heaven (Neh. 9:15, Ps. 105:25), the grain of heaven, and the bread of angels (Ps. 78:24-25).

used seventy-eight times in John's gospel. In eleven of these uses, John ties the idea of being sent (or coming from God/heaven) to the fact that Jesus was sent *into the world*.[19] For John *cosmos* is not merely a physical space, but also a metaphor for the condition of being lost, or apart from God.[20] Johan Ferreira concludes that while John's use of this word in his gospel is complex and multi-nuanced, the basic concept is best understood as that which opposes the sending of Jesus and the community.[21]

There are two implications from this for a church that sees itself as sent. First, the church exists as "sent" regardless of its geographic location. It is not only in the literal sending of workers to a foreign field that the church reflects its nature of being sent, but also in engaging the "world" wherever the church finds itself. In every geographic location, the church exists as sent. Second and related, the church is sent into an environment of lostness and blindness. This lostness is not contingent on geography. Wherever God places his people, they are guaranteed to be in an environment where light is needed.

Theological Implications

There are strong implications for thinking missionally about the church, and there are strong connections between this theological theme and our study of LST participants. Several passions flow from this new identity, and short-term missions can aid in the formation of these passions.

---

[19] 1:9, 3:17, 19; 6:14; 9:39; 10:36; 11:27; 12:46; 16:28; 17:18; 18:37.

[20] The word is used in this metaphoric/theological sense in 1:9; 3:19; 8:12, 23; 9:5; 11:9; 14:19, 22, 27; 15:18, 19; 16:33, throughout chapter 17 (17:6, 9, 11, 13, 14, 16, 18, 21, 23, 25), and 18:36. This double use of a word or concept is popular with John. Morris, *Jesus is the Christ*, 42, discusses briefly the use of multiple meanings in John and states, "John is a master at hammering away at his point from a number of angles." Ferreira notes that this word in John generally does not denote a physical or metaphysical reality, but is more of an ethical term. Ferreira, 109.

[21] Ferreira, 110.

Seeking Activity That Reflects Our "Sent" Nature

First, if it is central to God's view of his people that they are sent, we will seek ways of acting as his people that reflect our missionary nature. One of the reasons short term missions is important is not only pragmatics, but because it involves Christians in an activity that reflects their identity as a sent people. Because of this, God can providentially use LST workers who have poor motives or less than adequate preparation. Part of the task of ministry is not just to be busy, but to participate in a work that calls us to remembrance of our true identity in Christ.

Our observation of LST workers, though not without the possibility of bias, relates to the kinds of priorities its workers hold to as they leave a short-term mission experience and continue living and serving in the local church. One important theological question of our study is whether their work with LST will encourage them to participate in the life of the church in ways that reflect the true nature of God's people. Short-term mission experiences assist churches in helping their members affirm or discover their identity as a sent people by giving them opportunities for service that directly relate to the nature of the church as sent.

Short-term missions are also important because they actually shape workers into missional thinkers and doers. God is a sending God and wants his people to see themselves as sent people. The results of our study show that LST experience not only reminds people of their missional nature, but shapes them toward that character.

If the motivation for Christian service comes (at least in part) from a desire to be involved in works that reflect our sent nature, we will more easily steer away from involvement in ministry for less noble motives. LST workers should be motivated to go not because it is good for them, because they like to travel, because they have the money to do it, because they want to spread the English language, etc. LST workers go, in part, because they see themselves as sent by God. Our goal at LST is to always be driven by these deeper motives. The strength of any church's ministry will depend in part on the ability of those who serve to continually offer the "why" behind their actions.

Seeing All Activity Through A Missional Lens

Second, if we see ourselves as sent we will see missions as not simply a category of work, but as a way to approach all our work. It is a lifestyle. Here the question is, how can we look at what we are already doing, but view it through this lens of being sent? As we do this, we will begin to see that God's work is a round-the-clock kind of work, not just something we do when we gather on the weekend. Christians who consider themselves just "members" of a church will never be able to engage their community, their world, like Jesus did. However, those who see themselves as sent will see Jesus is calling our church to be in the world all the time.

This is an important realization because it addresses the issue of what happens for Christians who do not have the time, funds, or skill to participate in a missional activity like LST. Another way to participate in the "sent" nature of the church is by putting on new "glasses" and examining what we are already doing through a missional perspective.

Seeing Ourselves as Missionaries

Third, every member will see him/herself as a missionary. Part of the problem with the word "missionary" is that we tend to reserve it for those who are qualified by a unique set of gifts, experience, education, and funding to do the kind of work we consider missionary. If we are all sent, it means we all wear the label of missionary at some level. If we follow Jesus' lead we won't be content merely to send others out into the world. We will see ourselves, each individual, as sent into the world.

Our decisions to act as Christians must flow from a sense of who we are as Christians. The church will not engage its community nor become for God a saving presence in the world if it does not at some level see itself as distinct from the world but sent into it just as Jesus was sent.

Stepping Into Our Community

Fourth, if we see ourselves as sent, we will engage our community as a missionary engages his/her community. "Sent" implies a purpose, having to do with the way we interact with our context. A missionary church takes the initiative to engage its community rather than trying to maintain a fortress mentality. As God shapes workers into a missional character through short-term missions, he then uses these changed individuals to shape their local congregations and community. God wants his church (not only individual Christians) to see itself as sent. The results of this study of LST workers help us see that God is doing this through short-term missions. Local congregations are changing to gain the perspective of Johannes Blauw, "There is no other Church than the Church *sent* into the world."[22] Bosch correctly states,

> Mission does not proceed primarily from the pope, nor from a missionary order, society, or synod, but from a community gathered around the word and the sacraments and sent into the world.[23]

A theology of the-church-as-sent intersects this study because short-term missions are helping Christians gain a broader view of missions and the church in the world. Workers return understanding that regardless of their geographic location they are sent; they exist in the *kosmos* John refers to in his Gospel. John Stott calls for such a broader concept of mission in contemporary churches. In noting how mission is not only going across the sea to another continent, he writes,

> "I would also like to see regular vocation conferences, not *missionary* conferences only which accord the top priority to becoming a cross-cultural missionary, nor *ministry* conferences which concentrate on the ordained pastorate, but *mission* conferences which portray the biblical breadth of the mission of God, apply it to today's world, and challenge young people to give their lives unreservedly to service in some aspect of the Christian mission."[24]

Seizing Our Identity From the Proper Source

Last, if we are sent then we will take our primary identity from the one who sent us and not from the place to which we were sent. Jesus says that we are in the world, but we are not of the world. A

---

[22] Johannes Blauw, *The Missionary Nature of the Church: A Survey of the Biblical Theology of Mission* (New York: McGraw-Hill Book Company, 1962), 121.

[23] Bosch, *Transforming Mission*, 472.

[24] Stott, 33.

church that is sent will never completely feel at home in their culture. We do everything we can to engage our community and reach them, but we do not take our primary sense of identity from this place. We do not fundamentally belong to this place. Our primary allegiance and our actual home are with God.

This again addresses the motives of LST workers. Motive is informed by identity. LST workers do not serve because they are Americans, nor because they can teach English. At the core of their identity they are not simply Americans or teachers. They are children of God sent into a lost world, who just happen to be Americans with the ability to speak and an opportunity to share with non-believers in a unique way.

The church must learn to see herself as sent. We exist not simply as a sending agency. We exist as sent. When we capture this sense of purposeful identity, everything we do will change.

Chapter Five: Implications

There are strong implications flowing from this understanding of the church as sent and the short-term mission work that shapes us along those lines. As you have processed these short chapters we hope you have been thinking of what all of this means for you and your congregation. Each of us sits in a unique context with specific needs to address. Part of our prayer is that you will place that context and those needs against the truths coming out of this study.

However, we also know there are important truths here for all of us regardless of our situation. We think it worthwhile here to enumerate a few of the strong implications of this study.

Acknowledging the Power of Ministry to Shape

First and perhaps most obvious, short-term missions shape those who go, along missional lines. No ministry is ultimately done for the benefit of the one who serves. Service is done in Christ's name and for his benefit. However, this study shows clearly that God uses such service to shape his people and his church. God's people are returning from short-term mission work with changed hearts, stronger and more intentional hands, and a deeper commitment to His work in the world.

This realization calls us to question again what we are doing in our churches to intentionally help people become more like Christ. What tools are we using to help members become shaped more and more into the image of God? It is one thing for church leaders to be asking "What do our people need to be doing?" It is quite another for leaders to be seeking ways of helping church members *become* what God intends them to be. Of course, effective short-term missions are all about helping Christians DO effective ministry. However, as church leaders consider how to help their church BECOME more like Christ, we ought to consider short-term missions as a tool God will use to shape us (even as we seek to shape others).

It is worthwhile here to remember the scene that appears toward the end of Matthew's gospel (Matthew 25). Jesus paints a picture of a church very in touch with the needs of the world. They DID the right kinds of things; they –

Fed hungry people;

Quenched the thirst of those lacking drink;

Opened their homes to people other than their friends;

*Sacrificed in order to clothe those who owned
only the simplest of covering;*

Sat by the beds of those needing medical attention;

Visited those punished by society but still desperate for friendship.

Here is a group of people who did the right kinds of things. But notice what Jesus says will happen as they produce these actions – they experience the presence of Christ. Jesus says that when you do these things to others, somehow we do them literally to Him. Perhaps this is part of what Paul had in mind when he told Philemon to continue his ministry so that he would have an even fuller understanding of the good things we have in Christ (Philemon 4-6). Somehow we come to know Christ better when we serve in his name. Surely this is part of the change short-term workers experience as they serve. As they serve, they encounter Christ in ways perhaps previously unknown to them. Shaping Christians requires more than simply giving them the right kind of information or a culturally appropriate form of worship. Ministry shapes those who serve.

The Ripple Effect at Home

Second, because God is shaping his people this way, returning short-term workers are ripe for involvement in or initiation of any kind of work at their local congregation that is evangelistic or missional in nature. Some may be ready to help the church reach out to international people in their neighborhood. Others will want to join the missions committee. Some will want to teach about missions or get more people to go on mission projects. Still others will have new found interest in some form of long-term missions.

Due to this dynamic, local churches that are welcoming back returning short-term workers must take two actions. First, we must provide an environment in which new-found mission energy can be released. If returning workers come home and find no way to channel their energy for the lost, no encouragement to be involved, or little guidance in how to become involved, that energy will go unused or worse, dissipate. Strong and wise church leaders will prepare the congregation so that it can take advantage of God's work in these short-term mission workers. We will cultivate a church where such workers come home and readily find numerous ways to connect the church with its community or find support to jump back into cross cultural contexts and serve.

For congregations that are not yet connected with their community or with world missions returning workers will provide an excellent opportunity to begin such journeys. Will this be easy? Probably not. Any church that has taken the first steps of truly opening up to their neighborhood has experienced the challenging struggles that come with ministering to those who need Christ most. This kind of ministry can be messy! But, after all, wasn't Jesus' ministry somewhat untidy? Those who don't know Christ bring their broken lives into our church buildings for some serious rebuilding. This takes time, patience, wisdom, creativity, and a great deal of love. But what tremendous joy our churches experience when we begin reflecting the love of Christ for the world. This is what happens when our churches take seriously their call to re-present Jesus.

For congregations that already have open doors to the community and the world, the main challenge will be finding ways of getting returning short-term workers into these ministries. Are there walls or doors in front of our members who want to enter either leadership or just participation in our evangelistic and mission-oriented ministries?

- How easy is it for people to join the missions committee at our church?

- How quickly will the church fund a new ministry to immigrants in our neighborhood?

- How much public support from the church will members receive who want to start a neighborhood Bible study?

- How seriously will church leaders take the request of a member who participated in short-term work and now wants to consider long-term missions?

- How much encouragement will a returning worker receive to share her story with Bible classes?

Wise churches and church leaders will be looking for ways to craft doors rather than erecting and maintaining walls.

One might wonder about the duration of the excitement for ministry that returning workers bring with them from the field. We noticed in our study that returning workers are not simply on a spiritual high after their project. You might think that the excitement with which short-term workers return would quickly dissipate. However, we found that their energy and passion for God's work in the world doesn't go away quickly. For example, those who were farther away from the time of their first LST project perceived higher levels of positive impact on their life as a result of the short-term experience. As more time passed after their first LST project experience, worker's perception of the positive impact of this project rose rather than fell away. This simply means that the change God has wrought in the lives of short-term mission workers is ready to be released at home! Their passion will not evaporate in a few weeks. It may easily remain for years to come.

So, churches welcoming back returning short-term workers must provide an environment in which this new found mission energy can be released. These same churches must take a second action to adapt to returning workers who have been changed. Our churches will need to help some workers connect the dots between what they have just experienced and how God can use them now. Not everyone who returns will know exactly how to use their experience now that they have returned home. They may need help in allowing the transformation God produced within them to become something that affects their commitments and behavior upon returning home. In more than half the survey questions, those who had participated in their project 1-6 months ago scored the lowest positive change. That is, those who had just returned from their very first mission project seem to need help connecting the dots between what they just experienced and what that might mean for them now that they are home. They need help understanding what God did through them and how they have changed.

Another part of this same issue is realizing that such experiences affect men and women differently, and the young and old differently. Generally speaking, gender and age produce differing kinds of results in terms of how short-term workers experience change. Here are a few examples from our study:

- Women are more likely to indicate a change in Scripture reading and prayer (the first area of the study). This doesn't mean men did not indicate a positive change in how they read their Bibles and pray as a result of their mission experience. It simply means that women tend to indicate such a change more often and at a higher degree.

- Men on the other hand are more likely to indicate a perceived impact on their local congregation (the second area of the study). When they come home they seem to be able to see how their trip should affect their involvement in mission work at home.

- The younger a worker was when they first went on an LST project, the more likely they are to perceive a positive impact in their own life (questions in the first area of the study). Younger workers tended to see a strong personal impact from their mission experience.

- On the other hand, the older a worker is when they first go on an LST project, the more likely they are to perceive the positive impact of LST project experience on their local church in the area of missions.

- Women and younger LST workers evidently have a more difficult time perceiving a positive change in their local congregation as a result of LST project experience.

- Men and older LST workers have a more difficult time perceiving positive change in their own lives as a result of LST project experience.

All of these groups may need more explicit help to again "connect the dots." Women and younger workers of any gender may need assistance in seeing how their experience should affect their involvement in mission-oriented ministry at home. Men and older workers of any gender may need help understanding how their mission experience should shape not simply what they do at church when they return, but how God is shaping their own hearts as well.

These are just a few examples from the study. The main point is church leaders may need to intentionally help returning workers connect the dots. This could be as simple as sitting down with returning workers and asking them, "Now that you've had this experience how do you think God wants you to use this here? What does he want you to do? How does he want you to continue to change?" Even this kind of simple, straightforward questioning can help workers gain greater mileage from their short-term experience.

Bridging Short-Term and Long-Term

Third, local churches and short-term mission ministries must continue to build bridges from a short-term mission experience to potential long-term commitment. A percentage of people returning from short-term mission work are ripe for a call to step into long-term mission work. We must all look for ways of helping these workers take the next step along the path toward long-term mission work.

Some of our larger congregations may have enough resources (personnel, experience, finances, etc.) to actually help a member move from being a short-term worker to a becoming a long-term missionary supported and overseen by that same congregation. We know of one Texas congregation that sent an entire team of people to Mexico to plant congregations. Many of these workers were prior members at the sponsoring congregation. Church leaders used all their resources to train, equip, finance, and then send these missionaries. Perhaps your congregation has such resources and can have the incredible experience of sending to the field someone who has already been a vibrant part of the church's life.

Other congregations will not have the resources to pull this off. Such congregations can still participate in the joy of helping one of their own members explore their call to long-term missions. By partnering with other congregations and using the resources of other missions ministries and personnel they can walk with such members as they further test the waters.

This is not a call for local churches or even short-term mission ministries to become equipped to do all the vetting, training, and sending of long-term missionaries. Perhaps more important than that is the simple and powerful task of taking someone with a heart for long-term work and helping them know what to do next. If our congregation doesn't know the answer to "How do I become a long-term missionary" they should begin seeking answers!

Keeping High Standards

Fourth, because of the potential power of short-term mission work, those who plan such ministry should keep their standards high. Short-term mission work has changed immensely in the last 20 years. The training available to short-term workers today surpasses anything available even a decade ago. Some of the things we (LST) train our workers were unknown even to long-term workers in the past. For example, when every LST worker returns home we do some post-project training on how to report and how to handle reverse culture shock. We know of returning long-term missionaries who returned just a few year ago after being on the field for two decades and yet were never told anything about reverse culture shock! In fact because of the importance of training and the wealth of growing information about training for short-term mission we want to address this topic in the next chapter.

However, here it is enough to note that there is a new emphasis on quality and partnership. Those who go on short-term projects need vetting, training, and oversight. Our responsibility is to do the very best possible short-term projects. One implication of such responsibility is that not every local congregation should do short-term mission work unaided. Should we expect every local church to have all the necessary spiritual equipment to vet, train, and oversee short-term mission work? No. This is why we should continue to explore ways of partnering together so that every short-term effort is one of quality and excellence. A commitment to quality training and preparation should precede any commitment to keep things "in house." What is better, taking pride that a single congregation sent out one short-term team with no help at all, or that any congregation in any place can send a well-trained short-term mission team by using the help of other congregations/organizations?

Changing Our Minds

Fifth, one of the roadblocks to long-term mission work is a collection of misperceptions in the minds of those who should be considering such work. We know this because our study indicates that people are changing their perceptions about missions <u>as a result of</u> short-term projects. This means that prior to going they had some kind of incorrect perception about missions or their own participation in mission work. For example, the one question in this study that rated the highest positive change across age, gender, and time that had passed since their first LST project was the question "Has this experience affected your view and understanding of yourself in the area of missions?" Resoundingly people answered "yes." If more Christians are to consider long-term mission work they must believe that it is possible for THEM to do it.

If a Christian who has never done mission work does not believe they could ever do mission work we are already at a deficit when we start recruiting them! We should seek methods of removing such roadblocks from the minds of people so that when a call for ministry comes, their hearts are ripe for saying yes. It is true that some people simply need help gaining new skills before they will agree to consider mission work. Other potential workers have a deeper question – "Could God use ME to do his work?" If we could address this one question from a variety of sources and perspectives we might release armies of new workers ready to step out in faith and confidence.

Similarly, many Christians must capture a renewed vision of God as a sending God, of the kingdom of God as a place with no borders, and of what mission work actually entails. Some workers say "no" to the call for missions because they don't see God's global love, don't perceive his global work, and don't understand the incredible diversity of mission work around the world. We must attack these misconceptions with accurate and inspirational teaching, but also with quality short-term mission projects. One action we can take to replenish the supply of long-term workers is give more Christians an opportunity to experience short-term projects.

The way we think about ourselves, about the God we serve, about the nature of his people in other cultures, and about mission work matters immensely. As mentioned above, one of the most challenging obstacles to mission work of any kind is changing perceptions in any (or all!) of these areas. We realize that one of the most powerful things we can do for our congregations is shape their thinking in every one of these areas.

- What do I/my congregation believe about our role in God's global work? Can God really use me/us to make a difference?

- Do I believe God has a missionary heart? How global is his desire?

- Am I willing to admit that God's people are not only worshiping world-wide, but that their local congregations may look different than my local congregation?

- Is mission work simply one of the many good things our church should do, or is it something that characterizes everything we do?

- Are we senders, or are we sent?

Wrestling with these kinds of questions will provide not only ample opportunities for great discussions but may also help release the doubts, fears, and misconceptions of a potential army of workers.

Chapter Six: Training

Training for short-term mission work was not addressed directly in this study. However, it is not a great leap to see that there is a strong connection between our current study and the need for good training for all short-term workers. One of our assumptions in this area of change (based on 25 years' of experience) is that good training at the least means God has more room in the heart of a short-term worker to be at work. If a worker's heart is filled with doubt, with questions about their role on the field, and with an inability to understand or navigate a new culture, then God has less of the worker's attention. On the other hand, well-prepared workers will experience God in almost every aspect of their trip.

More and more congregations and mission groups are seeing the importance of and need for quality training. A search of books and articles written in the last decade about preparing for short-term mission will reveal a growing field of knowledge and experience. One of the more recent trends has been the adoption by a growing number of groups of "Standards of Excellence in Short-Term Mission." To encourage the pursuit of excellence in all short-term mission projects, a loose collection of short-term mission leaders and agencies in North America gathered in early 2000s' to begin creating a set of standards for short-term missions. These have become known as the "Standards of Excellence in Short-Term Mission." Close to one hundred sending agencies in the US have adopted the following standards.[25]

1. **God-Centeredness**

    An excellent short-term mission seeks first God's glory and his kingdom, and is expressed through our:

    1.1 **Purpose** — Centering on God's glory and his ends throughout our entire short-term mission process.

    1.2 **Lives** — Sound biblical doctrine, persistent prayer, and godliness in all our thoughts, words, and deeds.

    1.3 **Methods** — Wise, biblical, and culturally-appropriate methods which bear spiritual fruit.

---

[25] See http://www.stmstandards.org/ for more information.

2. **Empowering Partnerships**

An excellent short-term mission establishes healthy, interdependent, on-going relationships between sending and receiving partners, and is expressed by:

> 2.1 Primary focus on intended receptors.
>
> 2.2 Plans which benefit all participants.
>
> 2.3 Mutual trust and accountability.

3. **Mutual Design**

An excellent short-term mission collaboratively plans each specific outreach for the benefit of all participants, and is expressed by:

> 3.1 On-field methods and activities aligned to long-term strategies of the partnership.
>
> 3.2 Goer-guests' ability to implement their part of the plan.
>
> 3.3 Host receivers' ability to implement their part of the plan.

4. **Comprehensive Administration**

An excellent short-term mission exhibits integrity through reliable set-up and thorough administration for all participants, and is expressed by:

> 4.1 Truthfulness in promotion, finances, and reporting results.
>
> 4.2 Appropriate risk management.
>
> 4.3 Quality program delivery and support logistics.

5. **Qualified Leadership**

An excellent short-term mission screens, trains, and develops capable leadership for all participants, and is expressed by:

> 5.1 **Character** — Spiritually mature servant leadership.
>
> 5.2 **Skills** — Prepared, competent, organized and accountable leadership.
>
> 5.3 **Values** — Empowering and equipping leadership.

6. **Appropriate Training**

An excellent short-term mission prepares and equips all participants for the mutually designed outreach, and is expressed by:

> 6.1 Biblical, appropriate, and timely training.
>
> 6.2 On-going training and equipping (pre-field, on-field, post-field).
>
> 6.3 Qualified trainers.

7. **Thorough Follow-Up**

An excellent short-term mission assures debriefing and appropriate follow-up for all participants, and is expressed by:

> 7.1 Comprehensive debriefing (pre-field, on-field, post-field).
>
> 7.2 On-field re-entry preparation.
>
> 7.3 Post-field follow-up and evaluation.

While only the sixth standard above deals directly with training, it is clear that to meet all seven standards workers would need to receive training in wide variety of areas. This is just one example of the growing emphasis on training for short-term workers.

It is not the intention of this chapter to cover everything necessary for training short-term workers. It would be nearly impossible to do this given the huge variety of works that fall in the category of "short-term missions." However, by painting in broad strokes we think any short-term worker or leader will benefit from the following thoughts on training.

Backing into Your Training

Great training for short-term missions begins at the end. That is, one general principle to keep in mind as you think about training is to "Begin with the end in mind." It is tempting to start with the question, "What do we need to be training our workers?" A better question is "What does a well-trained worker look like?" Beginning with our end-goal in mind and then backing into that goal will help us be more certain of the outcome of our training. We need to have from the very beginning an image in mind of what the ideally trained worker will be like for this project, and then work toward that goal.

Here are some suggestions for doing this. First, create knowing-being-doing goals. Take some time to think through the following questions:

- In order to be an effect short-term worker on this particular project what will our workers need to KNOW (information).

- In order to be an effective short-term worker on this project what must they be able to DO (skills).

- In order to be an effective short-term worker what kind of person must they BE (personal qualities).

A focus on all three questions is crucial. If we focus only on action, then workers may serve in ignorance or with poor attitudes. If we focus on information, workers may not develop necessary skills prior to departure. If we focus solely on being the right kind of person we may end up taking a group of very nice Christian people who don't know enough to be effective and can't serve in meaningful ways. Giving our attention to all three areas helps us ensure a more balanced approach to our training.

Second make every part of your training tied to this "end in mind." If something in your training doesn't relate to one of these goals, cut it out. This is especially true with the growing amount of information available for training short-term workers. Everything you do in your training needs to be tied to one of your goals. Don't do something just because it sounds nice or seems fun. Make sure every aspect of your training is intentional.

Besides this focus on the end-goal of our training, great training also gives thought to the other side of training. We have to consider who is coming in to the training. Are we training adults or students? What do the people who are planning on going bring to the table as far as prior experience or current skills? We have found through many challenging situations that adults simply require a different kind of training than college students. So, to train both groups effectively we must give thought to not only the end-goal, but how to reach those goals from different perspectives.

Consider the group you are thinking of taking on a short-term project and ask the following questions:

- What do they already know or not know?
- How do they best learn (by information giving, by experience, with current technology or more "old school" methods, etc.?)?

- What can they already do or not do?

- What kind of prior experiences do they have?

- How socially, emotionally, and spiritually mature are they already?

As you answer these questions it will help you know how much preparation to do in each of the above areas. It will also help you know whether to screen out people that don't meet certain requirements in any of these areas.

This brings up an oft-neglected area of ministry- screening. One the one hand we want as many people as possible to serve on a short-term mission project. On the other hand, we know enough to realize that this kind of ministry is not for everyone. Screening potential workers might be considered a separate step from training, but it ultimately shapes the kind of training you will be doing. For example, if you bring into a potential short-term mission group some workers who are very emotionally/socially/spiritually immature you will have to constantly address that immaturity in your training.

The following diagram helps capture the kind of training system we are talking about:[26]

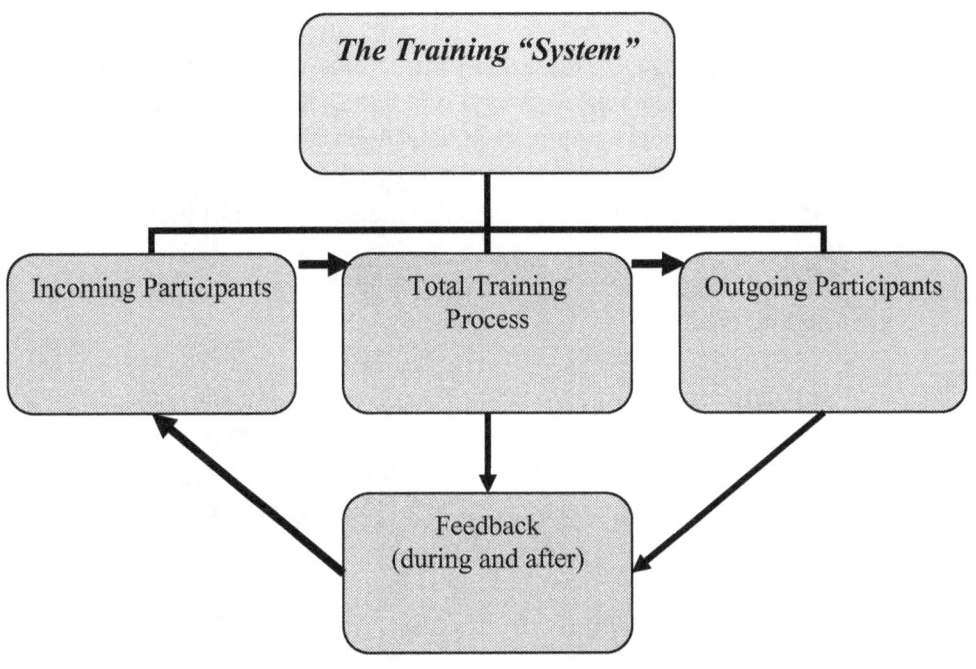

Training Areas

There are almost a limitless number of training areas one could consider in thinking through how to train short-term mission workers. For brevity and to keep the dialogue at a broad level, let's consider the following four areas as they relate to training. To provide uniformity to the discussion we will use the above model (knowing, being, doing goals) to address each issue.

Independence Verses Dependence

---

[26] I am borrowing heavily here from Clinton's work. See for example Robert, J. Clinton, *Leadership Training Models Manual* (Altadena, CA: Barnabas Resources, 1984).

The main issue at work here concerns how much of a burden the visiting short-term team will place on the inviting host. Ultimately every short-term worker is going to be a guest at that site and is thus going to be somewhat dependant on a host. The question is really how dependent will we be. One of the reasons this question is important is that our short-term projects should not burden the missionaries/hosts to such an extent that they start to cringe when they think of hosting the next group. Our projects should be a blessing to the lost, the local church, and the hosting missionaries. If they have to hold our hands every hour of every day for every possible need we are not blessing our hosts.

The following questions come into play when considering the issue of dependence:

- How large will our team be? (Those sponsoring short-term teams often want to take as many people as possible on one team. However, if we want our group to be somewhat independent on-site we may need to rethink the goal of taking large groups.)

- Where will our team live?

- How will we get around?

- How will we do laundry?

- Where will we eat?

- Where will we do our work, how will we get there, and will we need supervision while there?

- What kind of work will we be doing?

If screening is part of our training paradigm then this issue must be addressed even there. If independence is an important quality in short-term workers we need to screen for people who can be independent. We don't need to take people who are not self-initiators, who can't make decisions, or who are unable to function in new settings.

Knowledge

What kind of things will our group need to know in order to be more independent on-site? Do they need to know how to shop for their own food, to ride public transportation, to walk from their host-home to the church building, to get their own money exchanged, to make a call on a public telephone, etc? What kind of knowledge can we give our group to help them be more independent?

Skills

What kind of skills do we need in order to be more independent? Part of our training may need to include putting people in situations where they must practice being independent. How will our group make decisions while on-site? If there is just one decision maker, what happens if that person becomes incapacitated? What are we doing with our groups to make them practice group decision making prior to going? What kind of real-life scenarios can we give them prior to going?

Personal Qualities

What kind of personal qualities does an independent person have? What kind of attitudes do they hold? How does their dependence on God work itself out in terms of making independent decisions?

Training Example

Here are some examples of how we address these questions at Let's Start Talking. First, we intentionally send small teams (4-6 members) so they can live and work independently. It is much easier for a group of four to ride public transportation and cook for themselves than a group of twenty. Second, we screen for these qualities. We intentionally look for people who demonstrate the ability to live and work independently. Third, we ask our hosting missionaries to give an orientation to the team upon arrival so they can start learning to live independently. This includes a visit to the local grocery stores as well as instructions on riding public transportation. Fourth, we put our teams through experiential training which requires them to make decisions and work together prior to going. Last, we institute a form of leadership on all our teams that encourages shared decision making and responsibilities.

Objectives and Expectations of the Work On-Site

The issue at work here is what the team will actually do on-site. Having a clear understanding of the work the team will be doing can help you shape your training appropriately. When objectives and expectations are unclear it is more challenging to adequately prepare our workers.

A secondary, though still very important question, is how that decision was made. Who decided what would be done on-site? How much say did the local missionary and church have in deciding what the short-term team would do? The best short-term projects are those where the visiting team is conducting work which the host has invited them to do. If excellent training means we know the objectives and expectations of the work on-site, then we must begin this dialogue with the hosting missionary early enough to shape our training around those mutually agreed upon objectives. This means the leaders of a short-term project will need to begin dialogue with the local host months in advance of the actual project.

Knowledge

Once you've decided what your team will do, give thought to the knowledge goal. What do your workers need to know in order to effectively accomplish the work of the project? What information will help them most?

Skills

Second, what do they need to be able to do? What skills must they posses in order to accomplish the work before them? Then, how will we teach them those skills? Skills are built not only by giving our information but by providing opportunities to actually practice what will be done on-site. How will we work this realization into our training?

Personal Qualities

When I think about my team accomplishing "X" activity, what kind of person would do that well? What kind of personal qualities will they need in order to do the work effectively? Do they need to be able to talk openly and comfortably with strangers? Do they need to be good with kids? What kind of person will do well with this work?

Training Example

In Let's Start Talking our teams offer to help people practice speaking conversational English. This task shapes a good portion of their training. They receive regular instruction on how to do this, are given visual examples of what it looks like, and must practice before going.

Personal Qualities

The issue here concerns on a broad level the kind of person that will succeed in cross-cultural work. Often when a missionary reports having hosted an unsuccessful short-term project, part of what they will point to as being ineffective concerns the attitudes of the short-term workers/leaders. That is to say, one of the things that can make a short-term project really fly is not just what the team does but what kind of people are doing the work. The personal qualities that come to mind in this context are humility, flexibility, openness to learning, focused, selfless, etc. Are our workers going to be perceived as arrogant Americans or humble servants?

Knowledge

What information do our teams need in order to be this kind of team? One thing we see in training is that workers often need information in the form of specific scenarios to see why these personal qualities really matter. Some mission groups convey this kind of information by having teams sign statements which include a pledge to display appropriate personal qualities during the project.

Skills

What skills does a team need in order for these qualities to actually be at work on site? What skill is needed in order to maintain friendliness when you are tired? How do we practice patience when we are struggling with culture shock? How do we display thankfulness when we are eating foods we don't like? Practice dealing openly with tough situations and tough people prior to going. Put your teams in challenging situations prior to going then give them space to debrief and talk about them.

Personal Qualities

The personal life of the worker must be attended to prior to the project and not just during the actual work on-site. Screening again comes into play here. Look for people who display the kinds of qualities you think important. Then, make sure that this aspect of training receives as much priority as that concerning the actual work on-site. Think of the powerful way God will work when your team is not only impacting people through effective service but also demonstrating God's love in their own lives.

Training Example

In Let's Start Talking we give attention to this aspect of training in a variety of ways. First, we ask teams to conduct team devotionals prior to their project as well as while they are on-site. This is not something the team does as a preliminary to training. It is a core part of every training session. Second, we ask workers to sign a list of LST guidelines which include the kinds of behaviors we will exhibit on-site. Third, we use experiential training to expose people to difficult situations that require the demonstration of certain personal qualities. Then we ask them pull back from the situation and talk about how they should deal with it.

Long-term nature of our short-term work

One of the issues that is part of every short-term project is how our work will tap into the long-term work at that site. What are we doing to help make sure our work lasts as long as possible after we leave? Every short-term worker wants the effects of their work to carry on long past the date of their return home. To ensure this is happening we must tackle this issue long-before our team gets on the airplane for their project.

Knowledge

Does our team know how to connect their work to the larger work of the congregation on-site? Do they see how this project fits into the bigger picture? Do they understand the role of local church members in this project? The answers to these questions should be something all members of the team know. These answers are not to be shared solely among the leadership of a particular short-term project. Every worker should have a clear view of how their work is connecting with the long-term work of that site.

Skills

What components of our project require a skill from the team member in terms of tying this work more closely to the local congregation? If we are working closely with local Christians what skills do team members need in order to make that partnership more effective? If we are working with non-Christians in the community how are we tying them to the local congregation?

Personal Qualities

One of the tasks of our training is to help workers see themselves as part of a bigger picture. No short-term project should be an end unto itself. Similarly, no short-term worker should see the work that they do something that stops with them? How are we defining the role of a short-term worker to those wanting to travel with us? How do our workers see themselves in the larger context of this mission church?

Training Example

At LST one the main ways we approach this topic is by agreeing to work only with mission churches who have invited our teams to come and who agree to do successful follow-up of our projects. During the project itself LST worker spend time daily on certain tasks that will assist the local church in following up on their work. They record important information on Information Pages which will be left with the local host, they conduct a hand-off meeting with local hosts before they leave to ensure some local Christians know each of the Readers, and they conduct weekly social events to tie their Readers to local Christians through fun, neutral activities. Time is spent in training knowing how to use these Information Pages, how to conduct a hand-off meeting, and how to host successful social events.

Clearly a great deal more could be said about training. Remember that training is not simply passing on information. People are not trained who have only received information. They are trained when they have the skills, knowledge, and attitude necessary for the work ahead of them. We must constantly be aware of whether people are "getting it." Ask questions, use different teaching/communicating methods, be aware of gender needs as it concerns learning, etc. Even if all this chapter has done is raise your awareness to the importance of training we have accomplished a great deal!

Chapter Seven: Conclusion

Questions for further study

This study provides a window into the life of short-term workers from one mission organization and the impact that experience has on them. However, it also raises a number of questions. As we prepare to close this window into short-term missions, we believe you will benefit from at least listening in on the questions the study caused raised for us.

First, as a result of this study our own staff has made a commitment to conduct additional and regular institutional research. LST is already conducting research to build a demographic of LST workers (answering the question, "Who actually does LST?"). LST needs to conduct additional research into the impact the ministry has on local churches in North America as well as the effect of LST projects on the mission field. If the tools are available to further probe short-term missions with the goal of making them better, why not use them?

Second, all the areas explored in the interviews and survey could be investigated more in-depth themselves. For example, there is much more to examine in the area of how participation in cross-cultural ministry affects our reading and understanding of Scripture. What in particular makes reading Scripture in a cross-cultural setting so powerful? What does it take reading our Bibles through the eyes and culture of another person before we can see how much of our own reading is culturally conditioned?

Third, the effect of experience on theology can be explored more fully. Why does contemporary experience help us learn something new about God which we have not seen in Scripture? How does God reveal himself outside of Scripture? Are there aspects of God and his work in the world which some Christians will never know because they do not participate in certain kinds of activities?[27]

---

[27] That experience shapes one spiritually is well documented. Jean Blomquist notes the impact of divorce on spiritual formation. Jean M. Blomquist, "The Effects of the Divorce Experience on Spiritual Growth," *Pastoral Psychology* 34 (Winter 1985): 90-91. Barry James and Curtis Samuels demonstrate how high stress events shape spirituality. Barry J. James and Curtis A. Samuels, "High Stress Life Events and Spiritual Development," *Journal of Psychology and*

Fourth, there is a question about whether these results would be repeated in workers participating in non-LST short-term missions. Is there anything particular about LST that God uses to bring about the results in this study? Or, are the results produced by a dynamic that any short-term worker experiences regardless of whether they go through LST?

Fifth, what role does training and debriefing have on positive perceived influences? Do those who receive more training perceive a higher positive impact from the experience? Or, perhaps those who receive a certain kind of training will perceive such higher impact. These kinds of questions about training might yield important insights for any short-term leader.

Sixth, from the Christian spiritual formation field, one could question whether these results had anything to do with different age/life stages people go through and the growth that often accompanies those stages. Our study indicates that men and women, and younger and older LST workers, perceive different areas of change brought about by their LST experience. Is this difference due in part to life-stage?

Seventh, it is not clear what negative responses in the study indicate. Some participants indicated no connection between their

---

Theology 27 (Fall 1999): 250. In the field of religious education James Loder concludes that transforming moments need to be recognized as new sources of knowledge about God, self, and the world. James E. Loder, *The Transforming Moment: Understanding Convictional Experiences* (San Francisco, CA: Harper and Row, 1981), viii. See too Don Richter, "The Creative Process in Adolescent Development," in *Religious Education Ministry with Youth*, ed. D. Campbell Wyckoff and Don Richter (Birmingham, AL: Religious Education Press, 1982), 213; Edward Robinson, *The Original Vision: A Study of the Religious Experience of Childhood* (New York: The Seabury Press, 1983), 146; and Thomas H. Groome, *Sharing Faith: A Comprehensive Approach to Religious Education and Pastoral Ministry: The Way of Share Praxis* (New York, HarperCollins, 1991), 159-160. Theologically the area dealing with this phenomenon is practical theology. See for example Ray Anderson, *The Shape of Practical Theology* (Downers Grove, IL: Intervarsity Press, 2001). Scripture itself also supports the view that certain kinds of events are revelatory (Jn. 7:17; Mt. 10:40-42; 18:20; 25:35-36; 40, 45; Philemon 6).

LST experience and a certain area of life or ministry. However, this may be the case because they were already strong in that area (for example, having a mission oriented mind-set) and that is what drew them to LST. You have a chicken-and-the-egg dynamic at work. Are mission-minded people drawn to LST, or does LST produce mission-minded people? Or, negative answers may simply indicate that the worker did not perceive a positive outcome. These changes are occurring at a deep, world-view level. It may take months or years to perceive such changes.

Last is the question of how long-term these changes are. Our study explored the depth of change out to four years from the time of LST project experience. Would the same change be reported at further distances from initial project experience? Similarly, what results would we find if we did a longitudinal study, following the same group of LST workers over a 5-10 year span?

Closing Comments

God uses short-term mission projects to save his lost children. However, He also uses this activity to shape those he sends. This study has provided an in-depth look into the way God uses one ministry experience to produce a missional change in the workers, their priorities, and their commitments. Remember that we have only glanced at one side of the mission equation. Is it important that short-term workers actually make a difference in the lives of those to whom they were sent? Absolutely! Should short-term mission work be tied strongly to the long-term work of a local congregation at that site? Without question! However, because short-term mission work is little understood by most people, it is important to take a serious and studied look at this phenomenon. Our study in this book does not imply that the results found among this group of LST workers will be found in every short-term team. It does nonetheless provide powerful evidence demonstrating what God is doing in the lives and hearts of those who go. God is shaping not only individual people, but entire congregations through short-term mission work.

The theological notion that fuels this study is an understanding of God as a sending God. Because he is a sending God, he desires his people to view themselves as sent. The church is not simply a sending agency, but exists itself as sent regardless of its geographic location. As LST workers experience God's work in the world through LST projects they report changes which manifest a new-found appreciation for this theology. Once we see ourselves as sent (not just one who should send others) it is a short step to considering going into the world (or just our own neighborhood!) ourselves.

The motive for mission work can not be primarily centered on self ("I'm going because it is good for me"). However, the impact of an organization such as LST on long-term missions can not be measured simply by the number of people its workers baptize or in the amount of alumni who return to the field for longer periods of service. As we gauge the impact of short-term missions, we must also use studies such as this to examine the change in short-term workers when they return.

God needs workers committed for the long haul. For some this will mean moving to a new culture and operating in a new language. For others it will entail learning to open their own home to the neighbors right around them. For all, it entails the kind of missional mindset produced in many LST workers and articulated well by one such participant:

> *"I don't really see any distinction between being a Christian and being involved in missions. To me, they're synonymous. I mean every place is a mission because that's what we do; we have a mission as Christians. So it can be foreign or it can be next door, or wherever. It's all mission. It's all about people, not about things".*

Appendix: Exegetical issues related to the theme of sending in John 20:19-23

The first exegetical hurdle in this text is the question of whether these verses apply to all Christians or only to the original disciples or apostles. Ultimately, the answer to this question (and the other exegetical hurdles) is based in hermeneutics or theology rather than simple grammar or exegesis.

Few modern Christians restrict the synoptic Great Commission to a select group. Rather, it is regarded as a call to the church-at-large. Likewise, John 17 and 20:19-23 call all Christians to understand themselves as sent.[28] The sending language is so strong in John it almost defies understanding that Jesus intended his readers to pick up on it but not apply it to themselves. Newbigin believes that the mission on which Jesus sends the disciples in John 20:21 wholly defines the nature of the Church as a body of men and women sent into the public life of the world to be the bearer of that peace which Christ has wrought by the blood of his cross.[29]

There is a second exegetical hurdle in 20:21-13. If we grant that John 17 and 20 have application to the contemporary church in terms of seeing itself as sent, one of the tough spots in 20:21-23 is Jesus' statement about forgiveness. Prescott-Ezickson summarizes that it is generally agreed this statement of Jesus is not giving the church the prerogative of God. Rather, as the mission of Jesus is continued by the church, there is something about the mission that as people hear the message of salvation, they must make a decision. The

---

[28] Fenton Hort, for example, states, "The Twelve sat that evening as representatives of the Ecclesia at large." The apostles were representative of the entire church. Fenton John Anthony Hort, *The Christian Ecclesia* (London: Macmillan and Co., 1914), 30-31. Beasley-Murray, *Gospel of Life*, 115 quotes Hort, as does Lesslie Newbigin, *The Light Has Come*, 270. Beasley-Murray quotes Hort and says that the ones Jesus speaks to in 17:18 and 20:21 are representatives of the church that is to be; Jesus speaks to the church through the disciples. Raymond Brown likewise concludes, ". . . the Jesus of the Last Discourse transcends time and space, for from heaven and beyond the grave he is already speaking to the disciples of all time." Raymond Brown, *The Gospel According to John (XIII-XXI)*, The Anchor Bible (Garden City, NY: Doubleday and Co., 1970), 747.

[29] Newbigin, *The Light Has Come*, 268.

decision they make is what determines whether sins are forgiven or retained.[30]

On the other hand, after lengthy analysis, Raymond Brown concludes that there is not enough in either the Gospel of John or this specific text to determine exactly what is meant here, or to whom the power of forgiveness is extended.[31] Certainly, this part of 20:21-23 makes it challenging to see the entire passage as referring to the church as a whole, but there is enough evidence to make it at least seem possible.

The third exegetical item to note about this passage is the coming of the Holy Spirit in connection with the designation of the

---

[30] Prescott-Ezickson, 131. He states that if the disciples are the only ones sent, or the only ones authorized to forgive sins, then the rest of the church has no responsibility for mission. Since John was writing to a specific church, it would seem logical that he meant for them to pick up where the original apostles left off. Morris draws a similar conclusion. What Jesus does and says is to the entire group; the focus is not on individuals. Nothing in these verses necessarily indicates an individual has the ability to forgive or hold back forgiveness. And, even in the group, the focus is not on the apostles since in this passage it is only mentioned that the disciples are present (Morris believes it may even be the same group to which Lk. 24:33ff speaks). Additionally, Morris argues that the use of "anyone" indicates that forgiveness is something offered to a class of sinners, and that what is in mind here is not the forgiveness of individuals. He also notes that the verbs are in the perfect tense, seeming to indicate that the forgiveness is not actually something an individual or even a group is doing; it is a divine prerogative. Concluding, Morris states that the point is that the Spirit-filled church may say authoritatively, "such and such sinners have been forgiven. . .such and such sinners have not been forgiven." It is a declaration of what God has done, not of what the church is currently doing. Morris, *Jesus is the Christ*, 166-168. So too D.A. Carson, *The Gospel According to John* (Grand Rapids: Eerdmans, 1991), 655-656.

[31] Raymond Brown, *The Gospel According to John (xiii-xxii)*, 1045.

disciples (church) as sent.[32] This is an important part of John's sending theme. Gary Burge notes that in John there is a link between Jesus' continued presence with his community and the coming of the Holy Spirit. Just as Christ will be in the disciples (14:20), so too the Holy Spirit dwells with them and will be in them (14:17). For John, there is a great unity of Christ and the Spirit. The indwelling Holy Spirit is the indwelling Jesus. Jesus, though he is leaving, will not leave them as orphans.[33] No one is left to wonder if Jesus will truly be present with his people as they are sent. The disciples (and thus the church) are sent on the continuing mission of God with the continuing presence of God.

---

[32] Because Jn. 20:19-23 does not have an obvious parallel in the synoptics, there is a lack of clarity over what event this passage actually portrays. Gary Burge tends to parallel this passage and the events of Acts 2. Gary M. Burge, *The Anointed Community: The Holy Spirit in the Johannine Tradition* (Grand Rapids: Wm. B. Eerdmans, 1987), 117-149. Leon Morris leans toward viewing it not as the general outpouring of the spirit but as a specific ministry of the Spirit, the ministry of forgiveness. Morris, *Jesus is the Christ*, 165. D.A. Carson provides an excellent summary of several views concerning the Holy Spirit in this passage. In the end, he concludes that Jesus' reference is one of anticipation, not an actual outpouring of the Spirit. Carson, *The Gospel According to John*, 649-655.

[33] Burge, *The Anointed Community*, 137. See Jn. 14:18. On pages 140-142 Burge details the number of passages in John which parallel features of both Jesus and the Spirit. See also 15:26-27 about which Burge (page 204) notes that the mission of the Spirit and the mission of the church coalesce.

www.ingramcontent.com/pod-product-compliance
Lightning Source LLC
Chambersburg PA
CBHW020019050426
42450CB00005B/547